# THE REAL
# Spirit OF
# Revival

### PREPARING THE CHURCH
### FOR THE GLORY OF THE LORD,
### THE HARVEST, AND HIS SOON RETURN

## Bert M. Farias

# Contents

# Introduction

A number of years ago the Lord began dealing with me about writing and speaking on lost themes—truths in the body of Christ that have been understated or discarded but that need to be restored. *The Real Spirit of Revival* is a part of that assignment.

Some examples of such themes would include the end times, the rapture of the Church and the return of the Lord, heaven, hell, and holiness, the judgment seat of Christ etc. He said that there's got to be more preaching on these themes for they are emphasized in the holy Scriptures. He also told me that there has been a diabolical silence on holiness that has greatly weakened the character of the Church and opened a door to doctrines of devils.

The absence or dilution of these vital truths has created a large gap between the profession and practice of true Christianity in our day, and thus filled our society with much deception. The fear of the Lord which is the foundation of loving and receiving these truths is sadly lacking in the Church world today.

Have you ever asked yourself or quietly wondered why so many in the Church lack a strong devotion and dedication to God? Why are there so many professing Christians who still pursue the lusts and pleasures of the world? What kind of conversion experience does someone possess if there is no personal transformation or lifestyle change? These are difficult heart-searching questions that demand answers if we are to see change in our day.

Here are a few other questions to ask ourselves: Why is there such a disparity between Christianity in the book of Acts and what we are seeing today especially in the Western world? What caused people in the early Church to sell all their possessions and distribute the proceeds among those who were in need? In the midst of great persecution what enabled these first century Christians to continue to serve the Lord fervently? Where did the early apostles and the persecuted Church throughout the ages get the courage and the strength to continue to preach a gospel that was getting them beaten, tortured, and killed when the biggest struggle for many in the Western Church today is the fear of rejection and a need for self-esteem?

I strongly believe that the answer to all these questions and the cure to all the ills that face the Church today are to be found in personal revival in the lives of professing Christians. Without the holy fire of God burning in our hearts we will not be equipped to overcome the complacency, lethargy, and apathy so common in the Church world today. We also will not be able to endure the increasing spiritual warfare and antichrist spirit so prevalent in the Western world. Furthermore, it is the fire of God in our lives that will prepare us for the glory of the Lord and the coming harvest of souls, as well as the Lord's soon return. It is so critical in the dark hour we live in that we burn for Jesus!

The truths in this book are strong spiritual nourishment, and they have touched me and impacted my own life deeply. When someone is use to a light diet or an unhealthy dose of junk food it will take a little while to adjust to solid nutritious food again. But that's what the Lord wants for His people in this hour so they can be healed and strengthened, and then bear fruit that remains. May the Lord give you such a love for truth so that you will never again be afraid of confrontation and correction. The Lord chastens and corrects those He loves. His love is what gives us value and worth. *"Behold what manner of love the Father has bestowed on us, that we should be called the sons of God"* **(1 John 3:1)**!

Remember also that God never makes demands of you without empowering you to respond to those demands. He has sent us the Helper, the mighty Holy Spirit to aid us in every way.

God our Father holds nothing back from us. All that we need to live for Him has been given freely.

*"He who did not spare His own Son, but delivered Him up for us all, how shall He not with Him also freely give us all things"* **(Rom 8:32).**

The word "freely" in this verse is the same root word for grace. God gives grace. God graciously gives us all things. He equips us to receive His word and do it. It would be unjust for God to ask us to do something we could not do. This means that what God gives is never the problem. It's what we give Him. The heart and soul of revival is that God wants more of me, and that is the message of this book.

We all need more of His holy fire. If you've allowed the flame of His fire to grow dim in you, do not be discouraged, but put all your hope in God. He will ignite you again and empower you with great grace as you yield and submit your heart and life to Him.

Thank you for taking the time to delve into the pages of this book.

I give God all honor and glory for any blessing that it brings.

Let's pray:

*"Heavenly Father, I open up my heart and life to you. Have your way in me. Create a hunger in me. Light a fire in me. Grant me a spirit of wisdom and revelation that the eyes of my understanding may be enlightened. May the words of this book prepare me for your glory, for the harvest, and for your soon return. May I never be the same in Jesus name. Amen."*

# CHAPTER 1

# *Hardness of Heart*

*The most dangerous thing that happens in a church or a society is the hardening of people's hearts.* The battle of all ages from the beginning of time has been for the passions of mankind. In Jesus' own discourse concerning the end times He constantly addressed the condition of people's hearts as being the number one priority to watch over.

*"But take heed to yourselves, lest <u>your hearts</u> be weighed down with carousing (to indulge in extravagant pursuit of pleasure), drunkenness, and cares of this life (anxious about daily life), and that day come on you unexpectedly; for it will come as a snare on all those who dwell on the face of the whole earth. Watch therefore, and pray always that you may be counted worthy to escape all things that will come to pass, and to stand before the Son of man"* (Lk 21:34-36).

*"And then <u>many will be offended</u> (people's hearts), will betray one another, and will hate one another. Then many false prophets will rise up and deceive many. And because lawlessness will abound, <u>the love of many will grow cold</u> (people's hearts). But he who endures to the end shall be saved"* (Mat 24:10-12).

The apostle Paul gave similar warnings concerning the condition of people's hearts:

*"Now the Spirit expressly says that in the latter times some will depart from the faith..."* (1 Tim 4:1).

*"But know this, that in the last days perilous times will come: For men will be lovers of themselves, lovers of money, boasters, proud, blasphemers, disobedient to parents, unthankful, unholy, unloving, unforgiving, slanderers, without self-control, brutal, despisers of good, traitors, headstrong, haughty, lovers of pleasure rather than lovers of God..."* (2 Tim 3:1-4).

*"For the time will come when they will not endure sound doctrine, but according to their own desires, because they have itching ears, they will heap up for themselves teachers; and they will turn their ears away from the truth, and be turned aside to fables"* (2 Tim 4:3-4).

Other New Testament writers also reveal parallels between the end times and the condition of people's hearts being a major factor in the increase of sin and the departure from Christian morals, virtues, and values.

The Spirit of the Lord made this statement to me: *"Hardness of heart is the number one hindrance to revival."* If a person is not pursuing the Lord in their lives there will be some degree of hardness of heart in them. The prophet Hosea referred to hardness of heart as fallow ground (Hosea 10:12). Fallow ground is ground or soil that was once cultivated but has grown hard and barren and needs to be broken up or cultivated again. This describes the hearts of many believers in this hour.

Personal revival begins by looking at yourself and your own heart (1 Cor 11:31; 2 Cor 7:1; 13:5). We must examine ourselves and judge ourselves in the light of the Scriptures so we won't be judged and condemned with the world. The threat to personal revival occurs when Christians don't think they need to be changed.

In the Church today there is much deception because people have been made to believe that their entire consecration is not necessary for them to be followers of Jesus. Many have never been made to see the degree of hindrance their flesh is having on their spiritual lives. Statistics from recent surveys reveal that approximately eighty percent (80%) of the people in our churches today serve themselves. Many who attend Bible believing churches are there to learn to be a success in life and/or ministry, but so few really pursue the heart of God.

Charles Finney made the following quote: *"There is a certain type of Christian that although being constructively involved in the church and pass off as being very good Christians are useless in revival. I do not mean that they are wicked, but they have a form of piety which has no fire and efficiency and actually repels new believers, and wards off the truth."*

Personal revival births a holy enthusiasm and a fire in you. Could you keep silent if someone gave you a cure for all cancers, but told you not to tell anyone? If you really believed in the cure, you could not keep from sharing this with cancer patients everywhere. In the same way, when the kingdom of God touches your life you cannot remain silent. Jesus is the cure for sin and every damnable thing that would impoverish your life and spirit. Enjoying Jesus in your heart will automatically result in you sharing Him with your life and with your mouth. What is the depth of your personal response to the way Jesus has touched your life? That is how your love for God is measured.

*If you expect to make spiritual progress in your life you cannot bypass the thorough examination and evaluation of your own heart.* Are you on fire? Does your heart burn for Jesus? Are you hungry to know Him and to walk closer to Him? Is your heart tender? Do you weep easily when something precious touches your heart? Do you love and care for your brother? Do you love the lost and those without Christ? Are you filled with joy in worship because of God's presence? Do you freely express yourself in worship to God? Do you share your heart freely with loved ones? Do you hug your children and tell them regularly that you love them dearly? Do you do the same to your spouse? If you have difficulty answering these questions in the affirmative then you are not free. Your heart has been hardened.

*Keeping your heart is the biggest job you'll ever have on this side of heaven* (Pr 4:23). Anyone who has turned back from following the Lord missed it on this one point. Examine your life and heart thoroughly, be completely honest with yourself, or you will not make any spiritual progress. If you pile good works on top of the impurities of your heart, you will end up in further deception. The reason we have to deal with our hearts is because we must empty ourselves first before the Lord can fill us. Being filled with the Spirit of God is the position our hearts need to be in especially in these last days. That was the difference between the wise and foolish virgins (Mat 25). One group had enough oil and the other did not. God wants to anoint us with fresh oil (Ps 92:10) so that we will be strong in Him and we won't be easily distracted, diverted, or deceived by the spirit of this age.

The Lord is endeavoring to get Christians to pay closer attention to their spiritual lives because of what is coming on the earth. *We have robbed God not because we haven't paid our tithes and offerings, but because we have not given Him our lives.* If Jesus has your life and your heart He also has your money.

If you want to break up the fallow ground of your heart, you must begin looking at yourself through the mirror of the Word (Jam 1:23-24). The old timers preached this and would even go as far as instructing people to make a list of all their sins and shortcomings. They believed that this was a necessary part of dealing with a person's heart and breaking up the hardness. There is a place for this to be done today even in the light of our redemption and of the new creation realities of who we are in Christ. How easily things can slip into the closet of our hearts and become stumbling blocks in our fellowship with God! How easily wrong thoughts, attitudes, and motives can seat themselves in our hearts, and we are unaware of the damage they do. Allow the Holy Spirit to be your searchlight. Allow Him to reveal the issues of your own heart and to also empower change in you. Break up the fallow ground!

*"Sow for yourselves righteousness; reap in mercy; break up your fallow ground, for it is time to seek the Lord, until He comes and rains righteousness on you"* (Hosea 10:12).

In view of both the darkness on the earth and the coming rain of the Spirit, preparation of the soil is so necessary so that we can receive the full benefits of the rain of the Spirit. The rain will be lost unless the soil is properly cultivated. The rain can even be falling all around and yet not be producing in certain spots.

Soil that is hard cannot receive seed. There is fallow ground in our lives that needs to be plowed and cultivated. Soil that once produced fruit in the past can become crusty. Soil that was broken up last year can be wasted and lost this year. Many believers want personal revival without the plowing of the fallow ground of their hearts.

*The breaking up of fallow ground is not a one-time thing.* We need to constantly watch over the condition of our hearts. Abandoned and neglected soil receives no seed and produces no fruit.

There are preachers today who are out of the ministry who once used to weep with broken hearts for lost souls. Now they are angry and bitter. Persecuted churches in other countries wonder why American Christians never weep. There are churches that less than five years ago had the touch of God upon them, but today they are wastelands.

*A person can harden his heart without even knowing it.* Little foxes can get in and spoil your fruit (Sos 2:15). This is why it is so important to constantly evaluate the state of your heart. The heart can be deceitful. You can develop blind spots that keep you from seeing yourself as you really are. Others can often see what you can't see. I preached for years with great passion, but the Spirit of God showed me that I was hard-hearted in my preaching and in other areas of my life as well. It was a rude awakening for me to realize this. It has been said that before God makes a man, He will break a man. Like a coconut, in order to get the ingredients, the shell must be cracked.

It took several weeks of praying extensively in the Holy Ghost and fasting for the Lord to purge me of these things without me losing my boldness and intensity in God. And in order to keep what I've gained in the spirit there must continue to be a constant coming before the Lord. *Last year's brokenness won't do. Last year's burden won't do. Last year's vision won't do. Last year's plowing won't do.* To take new ground you've got to plow new ground. Putting the plow to your soul is painful but produces fruit unto holiness. And holiness is the habitation of God. When the heart is humbled you have broken up fallow ground and the Spirit of God can produce holiness in your life.

Communing with God from your heart helps you to break up that fallow ground and makes it increasingly difficult to stay hard in your heart. It is human nature to only call on God in your hour of trial when you have failed or when you need Him most, but you must learn to start out with God. Call on Him before you ever fall or fail. Call on Him before He sends the rain.

May the grace and peace of God be multiplied to you through the knowledge of the Holy One, God's most precious Son.

## CHAPTER 2

# *Personal Revival*

In the apostle Paul's writings to the churches he reminded them to "put off the old man" and to "put on the new man." If these Christians were new creations then why did Paul have to tell them to put off the old man, and not to lie, steal, be angry, use filthy language, etc. and to put on the new man with all its godly qualities (Eph 5, Col 3)? The apostle Peter also encouraged the early Christians to make their calling and election sure lest they stumble (2 Pet 1:10). The apostle John told the early Christians not to love the world (I John 2:15-17). Jude admonished them to "earnestly contend for the faith" (Jude 3). Why the constant admonitions to walk in righteousness, truth, and holiness to born again, Spirit-filled believers?

I praise God for the move of the Holy Spirit. I praise God for revivals that have promoted Christianity throughout the nations. I have found, however, that it is the daily life of Christians in their conduct and conversation that marks their relationship with God. It is so easy to slip into a mundane, complacent, and even sinful lifestyle unless these admonitions and times of both personal and corporate revival are frequent.

Some Christians need wake-up calls about every six months. I have seen them hot one day and cold the next. I have seen them excited for a little while and then discouraged and depressed later on. I've been there myself. We all need renewal in the Spirit. We all need personal revival.

While one of the primary purposes of grace is to make the saints of God conscious of their righteousness in Christ, the scriptures also admonish us to *"examine ourselves"* (2 Cor 13:5) and to *"judge ourselves"* (1 Cor 11:31) and to *"cleanse ourselves"* (2 Cor 7:1). The victory comes when you *"through the Spirit put to death the deeds of the body"* (Rom 8:13). *You* must put to death the deeds of the body, but it is through the Spirit that this is done. It is in *"beholding as in a mirror the glory of the Lord, that we are being transformed into the same image from glory to glory by the Spirit of the Lord"* (2 Cor 3:18). This means that the glory of the Lord in your earthen vessel is reflected and carried according to your understanding of the image of Christ.

Many times Christians confuse self-effort and works, with the grace of God. The image of Christ distinguishes between the two. *It is the image of Christ in you, the hope of glory* (Col 1:27) *that creates grace in you.* That grace is frustrated in you when you continually identify more with yourself than with Christ. Yes, while the Scriptures have much to say about the importance of works, you must understand that works born of grace and faith are the only works that are acceptable to God.

Still every believer is admonished to examine themselves and judge themselves in the light of Christ and the Scriptures. As I've said, personal revival is aborted in our lives when we do not believe we need to be, or can be changed. People have to be made to see that in order to be a true disciple they must make an entire consecration of everything to Christ. We need a revelation of the degree of hindrance our flesh is to the glory of God in us. The truth is that if we are not engaged in sanctification and the pursuit of God we will never experience personal revival. Grace is necessary and available for this. So what is the problem? *Our flesh!*

The problem has been that many know of their righteousness of God in Christ and that they've been saved by grace through faith, but they do not know how to apply grace and the help of the Spirit for transformation and personal revival.

How does one put off the old man and put on the new man? How does someone engage the Spirit in helping them with the infirmities of their flesh? How does one overcome bad habits? The answer is really simple: Feed your spirit and starve your flesh. Exalt the new nature in you. How do you do that? Just as physical exercise builds up your body so there are spiritual exercises that build up your spirit. There are at least five spiritual exercises that feed the new nature and build up your spirit while helping to mortify the deeds of your body.

1. The first one is *worship*. How much time do you spend in true private worship? Take time to worship the Lord in spirit and in truth. Present your bodies daily as a living sacrifice. Gladness and glory will fill your heart as you speak or sing to the Lord in psalms, hymns, and spiritual songs. (John 4:23, Acts 13:1-3, Eph 5:18-19).

2. *Meditation* is the second spiritual exercise that feeds our spirit. The wisest of men are those who meditate on the Word of God. Mutter the Word to yourself all day long. Begin to practice what you read and meditate on, and it will stay with you and become a part of your daily life (Jos 1:8, Ps 1).

3. *Confession* is a third spiritual exercise that affects our spirits and our souls. Closely associated with meditation, this tool will help to renew your mind and build faith into your spirit. As you begin speaking God's Word, you will build an image of the Word of God into your soul and you will begin to possess the promises of God, and the realities of your redemption (Jos 1:8, Mk 11:23).

4. *Fasting* is a fourth spiritual exercise that will greatly benefit your spiritual life. This is a purging tool. This exercise will help you overcome certain lusts of the flesh, strongholds in your mind and personality, and every sort of hindrance to your spiritual growth. It will also help you be in a position to set others free (Mat 6:16-18, Mat 17:14-21). In addition, your own health will improve (Isa 58:8).

5. The last spiritual exercise that will bring tremendous edification to your life is *praying in the Holy Ghost* or in other tongues. Tongues for personal edification is one of the greatest tools the Lord has given us for living the Spirit-filled life. Personally, I try and pray at least an hour or two every day in the Spirit. You may want to start with 30 minutes until it becomes second nature to you. I'll guarantee that there will be an exaltation and a sensitivity in your spirit unlike anything you've ever known. Your inability to produce spiritual results in your life will be removed (1 Cor 14:2, 4) (Jude 20)!

If you have little to no desire to incorporate these practices into your life, I suggest you go through a time of sincere repentance from sin, idolatry (loving the world), apathy, and complacency. If you have lost your desire to pray, read the Word, and witness for Christ, then you are in a backslidden condition. Call on the blood of Jesus. There is mercy for your sin and failures, and grace to help empower you to victory in a time of need (Heb 4:16).

Remember, God cannot do anything about your flesh. He told you to do something with it. These five spiritual exercises are the way to get there.

# CHAPTER 3

# *First Love Lovers*

Jesus said that His Word would judge everyone who rejects Him and fails to receive His words (John 12:48). Conversely, His Spirit is like a fire that burns the present hour speaking of His Word into our hearts.

Rev 2:1-5 is such a word. This message of returning to your first love is an end-time theme and one the Church so desperately needs.

The church at Ephesus possessed some noble characteristics. Jesus commended this church for many things. By today's standards this church would be thought of as a strong and even dynamic church. They had doctrinal and moral purity, labored without growing weary, the people were active in the affairs of the church, had exercised patience and perseverance etc., but there was one thing Jesus had against them; they had forsaken their first love. Jesus called this position a fallen place or in today's terminology, a backslidden state. What a lesson to learn that Jesus, the Head of the Church, does not see as man sees.

What does the Lord of glory see in today's churches? What of those who boast in great attendance, occupy large buildings, and have dynamic programs for their members? Jesus does not esteem things as a man esteems them. He so often regards as least that which men esteem highly. On the other hand, those things that men often esteem lowly are so highly regarded by the Master. You see, it doesn't matter what size building, attendance, or organizational powers and abilities a church possesses. If first love has passed, then it is a fallen church, and one in danger of having its lamp-stand removed from its place (Rev 2:5).

The lamp-stand represents the church, and the stars are the angels (Rev 1:20). Every church ordained by God has an angelic covering that symbolizes the power and anointing for that church to operate. The lamp-stand being put out represents the angel leaving and being assigned elsewhere. There are churches that still exist today whose angel left 100 years ago; sad, but true. There is no longer a covering or an anointing for that church to operate. They lost their love for Jesus. Over a period of time religion had hardened their human spirits and left the hidden places of their hearts untouched. Thus, intimacy with Jesus was lost, and by failing to make the adjustment the church lost her power.

Religion is the crowning work of Satan. He works to extinguish the intimacy of the Lord from our lives so that everything we produce comes out of works not born of love, but of duty. These are dead works. The spirit of religion always causes us to produce outside of the new nature, which is love. This results in a form without the power. Falling in love with Jesus and staying in love with Jesus is your sure foundation for protection against the deception of having a form without the power.

The apostle Paul's heart cry to know Jesus (Phil 3:10) was like the loaded gun he carried in life and ministry. He called it a prize to be won. Here is a man who had come to visions and revelations, some not to be uttered…he had come to a place of great power in ministry where handkerchiefs were taken from his body and placed on the sick and demon possessed, and the diseases and demons left them…angels had visited him…mighty churches were raised up by him…and nearly two-thirds of the New Testament was written by him. Yet, Paul's chief aim was for the prize of knowing Christ, and having a privileged seat next to Jesus for all of eternity (Rev 3:21). Do you want that seat?

Not all saints will sit on thrones in the holy city (Rev 20:4). That beloved city is the Bride of Christ, called the New Jerusalem (Rev 21:2). It is the wise virgins, the first love lovers, who will receive that privilege. No wonder Paul was so passionately consumed with being a first love lover of Jesus. Within the realms of that love is an eternal glory, position, and ranking which shall never be taken away.

First love lovers are those who have stayed close to the heart of Jesus thereby keeping their vessels full of oil and their lamps burning bright (Mat 25:1-13). Their first love produced first works that translate into gold, silver and precious stones, which are in turn, used as building materials for our eternal home. The New Jerusalem is an ongoing construction project being built from the works of those who lived surrendered and consecrated lives to Jesus. Thus the reason for the call to the church of Ephesus to repent and return to her first love so that she might do her first works (Rev 2:5). Are these words burning in your heart yet?

There will be sorrow and regret among many saints for the wood, hay, and stubble that will be burned up at the judgment. Their works, when tested by fire, will be found wanting. What would Jesus find today in many of our prominent churches and ministries across the globe if all our works were exposed? With fear and trembling we must serve the Lord. Jesus is at the door.

The mountaintop Christian life is one of first love. Anything short of that is a fallen state (Rev 2:5). From that heightened place of first love flow all first works. This is a great position of power. It is a place of sometimes almost silly but such pure delight. This is such a lovely place to be, a place of continually beholding the face of Jesus, of seeing His glory with the eyes of your understanding, of blessed rest where nothing un-nerves you.

You can buy this place with no money. You can pursue it without any earthly craft or ability. It is not a place exclusive to anyone above another. It is purchased with your heart only. It is purchased with a spiritual hunger for living bread, and thirst like a deer that pants for the water. It is a place available to the lowest status human being on the earth as well as the rich who will encounter difficulty in pursuit of this prize. Can you count the cost as Paul did? Count all things dung for this holy knowledge? Cast aside all other pursuits? How much is it worth to follow the Lamb wherever He goes throughout eternity (Rev 14:4)? Do you want that seat (Mat 20:21)? Will you enter into that holy city (Rev 21:2)?

Behold the Bridegroom cometh!!! Are you His bride in patient waiting? Do you long for His face? Is He your first love? If not, remember from where you have fallen, and repent and do the first works. If true repentance works its course, in the end the glory revealed shall be so much greater than any of your present sufferings.

All the love of our glorious Bridegroom is backing the pen of this ready writer. May He bless these words to your ears, and multiply His grace in your life to love Him.

# CHAPTER 4

# *Be Filled with the Spirit*

At the return of Jesus the greatest difference between the wise and foolish virgins as illustrated in Matthew 25:1-13 is that the wise will have extra oil, but the foolish will not. Oil, of course, is a type of the Holy Spirit. The wise virgins were ready for the coming of the Bridegroom because they were filled with the Spirit, but the foolish, though they knew about the Bridegroom's return, were not ready because they did not maintain an infilling.

The number one priority in these last days in the Church is not evangelism; it's not discipleship; it's not prayer, fasting, and giving. These things are all very, very important, but the number one priority on God's heart for His people today is to maintain a fresh infilling of the Holy Spirit. If you are filled, then evangelism becomes your breath, discipleship becomes your heartbeat, while prayer, fasting and giving becomes your life. These things all flow from being continually filled with the Holy Spirit (Eph. 5:18-19).

*There is a diminishing ability in the body of Christ today to draw from the Spirit of God.* When the body of Christ is ruled by the flesh, filled with the spirit of the world, and governed by the philosophies and traditions of men they extinguish their ability to draw from the Holy Spirit and thus live far beneath their God-given privileges.

There is a spiritual law that says: The more you yield to the Spirit the easier it is to yield, but the more you yield to the flesh, the easier it becomes to keep yielding to the flesh. Some of us need to reverse what or who we've been yielding to. *Every time you drink of the flesh and the world you diminish your ability to drink and draw from the Spirit of God.*

Old Testament scriptures are sometimes used to attempt to bring the promise of the Spirit who has already come. We pray for an outpouring, but God says to be filled with the Spirit. We pray for the fire, but God says to be fervent and fan the flame of God within you (2 Tim. 1:6). In other words, we are to activate what is already in us. You are the temple of the Holy Spirit!

*The Spirit-filled life is offered by grace in the New Covenant and not the law of the Old Covenant.* The law makes us conscious of our sin, lack, and inability while grace makes us conscious of God in us. We need to get out of the shadow of the law where the death nature governed the actions of men, and get on into the light of New Covenant living where the life of God now reigns. The Old Covenant has been given to us for an example, but it has been fulfilled in the New. This is a problem for many people in their understanding, and it keeps them out of the grace of a Spirit-filled life.

How do we maintain a Spirit-filled life? It all starts with an attitude of praise and thanksgiving. Thankful people are full people. Thankful people are unselfish people who look out for the interests of others.

When you take your eyes off yourself and your problems you will begin to rise in the Spirit, but as long as you maintain a self-focus you will continue to sink lower. God's nature is unselfish. As you learn to live a life of praise, your thoughts toward others will be God-thoughts because of the infilling you receive through your praise.

The way to be full of the Spirit is to start every day in the Spirit. Then keep your heart turned toward the Lord all day long. In other words, carry the increase of the Spirit gained in private fellowship, and operate in it throughout the day. Filling up privately starts with praise and thanksgiving. It begins by praying in other tongues and letting those tongues launch you into psalms, hymns and spiritual songs, not from a song book but from your recreated human spirit. These are inspired utterances that come from the depths of your being. We must learn to fine-tune our spirits and draw from the Spirit of God. If you're not used to communing with the Lord this way, it will take you a little while to get it going, but through exercise you can develop your spirit until you learn His touch. Some believers have never learned to drink from the Spirit of God. Others have been out of fellowship and need to re-learn some things.

Many Christians today are confusing yesterday's momentum with today's infilling. So many who used to be on fire and fervent in spirit are now cold and dry. Actually, spiritual momentum can decrease so gradually and people be slowing down without even knowing it until they are running on empty.

All kinds of things in this life will try and empty you out. Trials, tests, and adverse circumstances will come against you, but opposing forces can never penetrate a full man. They bounce off him. Jesus went into the wilderness full of the Spirit, and after being tempted and tried He came out in the power of the Spirit (Luke 4). *To a full man opposition is an opportunity to grow in power.*

Think of the capacity of a man's spirit and the amount of power it can contain. The mad man of Gadara whom no man could bind even with shackles and chains and whom Jesus delivered had 2,000 devils. If a man's dead spirit can contain 2,000 devils and survive, think of how much a man's born again spirit can contain of God's presence and power! Just as there is no bottom to sin, symbolized by the 'bottomless pit,' there is no ceiling for the glory of God in the opposite direction. How much of God do you want? You can drink all you want. There is no excess in the Spirit. You can't drink too much of the Spirit of God. There are no limitations to how full you can get.

*We need the infilling of the Holy Spirit more than anything else in our day.* We are to pray in the spirit, rejoice in the spirit, worship in the spirit, walk in the spirit, and live in the spirit, as this is God's New Covenant plan. The devil attempts to bring in the old order with all its legalism and tradition to diminish the newness of the Spirit in our lives and what that could accomplish. But let's rise up in the newness of our spirits and develop ourselves to a place of power and victory. Learn to connect your tongue to your spirit and speak life, blessing, and praise from that place.

*Living full of the Spirit is the perfect position for God's highest workings in your life, and it is the remedy for every imperfection.* To be full of the Spirit means to be full of God and all that He is. How can you improve on that?

As we get closer to the rapture and the return of Jesus, our preoccupation should be more on being full of the Spirit than anything else.

Take time to practice Ephesians 5:18-19 and Col 3:16 and develop your spirit in these things. Stay in the Word, but give place to speaking and singing God's praises supernaturally.

*"And they worshiped Him, and returned to Jerusalem with great joy, and were continually in the temple praising and blessing God. Amen"* **(Luke 24:52-53).**

*"As they ministered to the Lord and fasted, the Holy Spirit said..."* **(Acts 13:2).**

Wise virgins are anointed with fresh oil. This is why they will be ready when Jesus comes.

## MIRACLE WINE

Oil is a type of the Holy Spirit, but so is wine. At the wedding in Cana, when the command was given to fill the 6 water pots with water at the appointed time (John 2:7-8), then and only then, appeared miracle wine. Each water pot measured 20 gallons for a total of 120. And so it was in the upper room when 120 human clay pots, disciples of the now resurrected and ascended Lord Jesus, would gather and wait for the appointed time when they would receive miracle wine and power from on high (Acts 2).

And when the fulness of time came, the sound of a mighty rushing wind was heard and cloven tongues of fire like lightning sat on each one of them (Acts 2:2-3). "Draw out now and pour the water into these human clay pots!" proclaimed the governor of the feast. Then out of their bellies flowed rivers of living water that suddenly turned to miracle wine, just like at the wedding of Cana in the beginning of Jesus' ministry. And so the show began!

Down from that upper room came that new creation of drunks stumbling and staggering from days filled with praise and now proclamation of the wonderful works of God. Divers kinds of tongues from other nations did each man speak, not having learned but yielding their tongues to utterances hitherto never spoken. In times of old God confused languages of men so that their one tongue could not unify them for evil (Gen 11). Now divers tongues of men and of angels would unite men for good. How marvelous is our God!!!

Some men were amazed and perplexed by this strange phenomena while others mocked, saying, "these men are full of new wine!" But Peter lifted his voice and exclaimed, "these are not drunk as you suppose... but this is that which was spoken by the prophet Joel" (Acts2:12-16)!

This is how God chose to pour out His Spirit and introduce His glorious Church to planet earth! Jesus began His ministry this way, and the New Testament Church began this way, too! With miracle wine!!! What do you think of that? It tells you something about our God, does it not? He is the great bartender! The table He sets is governed by the Holy Ghost. He likes His people to be drunk with joy unspeakable and full of glory!!!

Come to the table of the Lord!

This is a great dynamic that the Lord desires to re-introduce to His people in this hour. It is the DRUNK CHURCH! Filled with praise... filled with power...filled with glory! As the world succumbs into more darkness and despair the true Church will shine with the glory of the risen King! Many will again be amazed and marvel while others will continue to mock.

The governor of the feast saves the best wine for last! These are the last days! Let's get filled with the Spirit to overflowing! Let's get drunk!!!

## ARE YOU LIVING IN PSALM 126 OR 137?

And the Lord said to me, "Make sure you are living in Ps 126 and not 137." In 137 the children of Israel are in captivity and have no joy, laughter, or song in their hearts. But in 126 they are full of joy and gladness and the spirit of prayer (weeping), and they are working in the harvest and reaping the fruit of it.

Many are in captivity now, but for those who will stay close to Jesus He will be to you as the governor of the feast who turned the water into wine and saved the best wine for last. As in John 2 also in Acts 2; water turned to wine! Rivers of living water coming forth from their bellies turned into wine.

And so the oil of joy is flowing and the wine of the Spirit is being served. Those who love righteousness and hate iniquity, as the Son did, will be anointed with gladness more than their companions (Heb 1:9). The glory of the Lord will shine on the true Church, the Bride of Christ, and she will do exploits.

There is a line of distinction that has been made. Ps 137 or Ps 126? Which side are you on? Those in 126 are going up, but those in 137 will stay. One will be taken and the other left (Mat 24:36, Mat 25:1-13). As the time approaches the governor of the feast will continue to serve up the new wine. The saints will be marked by righteousness, peace, and joy in the Holy Ghost (Rom 14:17). The kingdom shall be manifested through them.

Come out of captivity and get into the flow of the Holy Ghost and of Ps 126! Be filled with the Spirit!!!

## CHAPTER 5

# *Sweet Surrender*

*Then he said to them all, "If anyone desires to come after Me, let him deny himself, and take up his cross daily, and follow Me"* (**Luke 9:23**).

The pathway to real discipleship goes through Luke 9:23. You cannot follow in the footsteps of the Master without the application of these words that flowed from the lips of Him who subjected Himself to the Heavenly Father in the same way.

In His earth walk Jesus presented Himself as a daily offering to the Father. This was the pattern He set. This was the key that unlocked the door to the room of fellowship Jesus experienced and enjoyed with the Father each and every day. And Jesus has called each of His followers up and into that room. Luke 9:23 is the door!

The cost to access the same room of fellowship Jesus accessed each day of His life is nothing short of full ownership. *"And He died for all, that those who live should live no longer for themselves, but for Him who died for them and rose again"* (**2 Cor 5:15**). It's perfectly fine to love life (2 Pet 3:10) as long as it's not your *own* life (John 12:25). There is a place of death and life where Christ reigns in the body.

What a lovely place to be in! From an earthly perspective and to the carnal mind this may seem like a grievous thing to deny yourself and take up your daily cross, but this is only because you have not fully understood the measure of hindrance your flesh has imposed upon the life of Christ within you. If you have only tasted the old wine you will not really know how much better the new wine is. Luke 9:23 is the doorway into the new wine of fellowship with the Trinity. Once you get in and you lose your life you will gain another. You will move from the natural into an amazing grace. The Spirit will begin to work a meekness of the Lamb of God into your soul.

If you want what is on the other side of the cross you've got to go through Luke 9:23. When you do, then love will transform you. The Spirit of God will begin to purge you of the things of the flesh and the blood of the Lamb will cleanse you. You will be more one with the Lord. This is the way to come into agreement with the perfect will of God. Anything less than this crucified walk will produce an unsanctified mixture of the flesh and worldliness in your soul that is not conducive to life in the Spirit.

The beginning of our transformation comes only when we come to the end of our own self-sufficiency. It is that ministry of death that leads to life. You, through the Spirit, must put the flesh to death daily for the flesh can never please God. Even Jesus had to spend nights alone with the Father to stay in that blessed place of submission. You can be a disappointment to the Lord if you become lukewarm and complacent and stay in a place where sin and the flesh have the ascendancy in your life. Be ever so watchful and careful of coming under the influence of a self-pleasing spirit where you draw back from a whole-hearted and complete devotion to Jesus.

You cannot bypass the cross. There are no shortcuts. There has been a general superficiality of the gospel in our culture that deceives us into believing that we can attain to great spiritual heights without going the route of Luke 9:23. If you believe this you are putting yourself above the Master (Mat 10:24-25).

Was it not Jesus who said that He could do nothing of Himself (John 5:19)? Was it not Jesus who said that He came not to do His own will, but the will of the Father (John 6:38)? Was it not Jesus who learned obedience even through the things which He suffered (Heb 5:8), becoming obedient even to the death of the cross (Phil 2:8)? Are we more than the Master? Are we better than He was in His earth walk? Are we not called to live as He lived and to follow in His steps (1 John 2:6, 1 Pet 2:21)?

Where are the signs of this cross-walk in the body of Christ? And where is the message of the cross in our gospel? Recently I heard of a major Christian media consultant who said that the reason for the lack of substance and weighty messages on Christian television today is because the average viewer doesn't have an appetite for it. Most only have an appetite to hear how wonderful they are, and how rich and blessed they can become. If the cross were preached, viewers and funds would be lost. What are these money-minded ministries building? Telling people what they want to hear instead of what they need to hear is wood, hay, and stubble. This should fill our hearts with great sorrow as it does Jesus.

When a well-known minister was allowed by Jesus through a prophetic vision to speak to the apostle Paul, Paul said there were two things that the Church attained to in his time that they quickly lost and must be recovered today. "You must recover the ministry and the message." Here is his explanation of that statement.

*"Except for a few small places in the world where there is great persecution or difficulties now, we can hardly recognize either the ministry or the message that is being preached today. Therefore the Church is now but a phantom of what it was even in our time, and we were far from what we were called to be. When we served, being in the ministry was the greatest sacrifice that one could make, and this reflected the message of the greatest sacrifice that was made—the cross. The cross is the power of God, and it is the center of all that we are called to live by. You have so little power to transform the minds and hearts of the disciples now because you do not live, and do not preach the cross. Therefore, we have great difficulty seeing much difference between the disciples and the heathen. This is not the gospel or the salvation with which we were entrusted. You must return to the cross."* (Joyner, The Final Quest)

How relevant is this word of wisdom from the Lord for the hour we live in today! The Church needs to awaken and respond to such a word.

How do you get to this place? And how do you respond to this word? Once again, Luke 9:23 is the door! Let's go through the process.

**"If anyone desires to come after Me..."** First there must be a desire, a hunger to follow Jesus closely and to know Him; a hunger for the perfect will of God, and for the presence and power of God. Spiritual hunger is a precious attribute and will get you into high places in the Spirit. Hunger and desire will make a man do extreme things. John G. Lake, that great apostle to South Africa earlier in the 19th century, spoke of a time in his life, even before his ministry in Africa, when his soul was demanding a greater entrance into God.

*"There was such a hunger for God that as I left my offices in Chicago, and walked down the street, my soul would break out, and I would cry, 'Oh*

*God!' People would stop and look at me and wonder. I felt myself on the borderland of a great spiritual realm, but was unable to enter in fully, so my nature was not satisfied with the attainment..."* John G. Lake

Don't be satisfied with what you already have because there is so much more. It is good to possess a divine dissatisfaction in your soul. It is well pleasing to the Lord to stir up your hunger and desire for more of Him. Get alone with God. Don't just read the Word of God, but let the Word read you. Let the words of Jesus become your living bread. Add some fasting to your prayer life and walk with the Lord (that is a big part of denying the flesh). Worship Him on your face. Wrestle with God if need be. I believe one night alone with God, as Jacob spent, could transform you and restore the ascendancy to your spirit, and make you too, a prince with God.

Secondly, **"Let him deny himself..."** In other words, deny your flesh and your un-harnessed soul (Rom 12:1-2). Again, fasting with the right motive is a big part of that (Mat 6:16-18). The body and the soul must surrender its authority and dominion every day or else it will become more and more difficult for you to get into the realm of the Spirit. You are either going forward or backwards each day, promoting or postponing what God really wants to do in your life. Initially there will be a battle in your will where the seat of your decision-making lies. Your emotions will give you fits, and things will seem dry at first.

This is where many Christians falter. That dry process is a result of the ascendancy that your flesh has had over your spirit for some time. The dryness is nothing more than the change you're going through. What makes you think that just because you don't sense God that He is somehow not pleased with you, or that you have not broken through? Dryness has nothing to do with whether or not you've broken through.

In fact, some of the times you feel His presence less are the times you've actually broken through more because you're dealing with hindrances that before kept you from seeking Him. This is the pathway to your personal transformation and into the glory of His presence.

*"The way into glory is through the flesh being torn away from the world and separated unto God."* Smith Wigglesworth

Wigglesworth books are often-read books of mine. I like to follow 100-folders (Mk 4:8, 20), but he wasn't always a 100-folder. It wasn't until his later years when he came into it. Wigglesworth was actually in a backslidden condition for a number of years when he would frequent the bars and drink and forbid his wife to go to church services. He was very cantankerous and hot-tempered until he got alone with God, and entered into the condition of full surrender. God led him to know that he could never be of service to Him until he was wholly sanctified.

Surrendering to God and living a life of purity and faith was the response that Wigglesworth would give to those who wanted more of God.

*"When God brought me into a deeper experience with Him He spoke by the Spirit making me to know I had to reach the place of absolute yielded-ness and cleansing so that there would be nothing left."* Smith Wigglesworth

I know that this is not a popular message today, but it is one of the greatest secrets to a deeper life in God. Why do you think there aren't many men like Smith Wigglesworth and John G. Lake walking around the earth today?

Here is the final piece to Luke 9:23:

*"And take up his cross daily, and follow Me."* The daily decision to either walk in your own will or submit to the will of God is your cross. In Jesus' most trying hour in the garden of Gethsemane, before going to the cross, He prayed and submitted His will to the Father. *"Oh My Father, if it is possible, let this cup pass from Me; nevertheless not as I will, but as you will."* Jesus submitted His will to the Father every day, but now He was facing the most difficult trial of His earthly walk. Jesus did not just pray, but He surrendered His will. You can pray for hours and surrender nothing. Many Christians pray, but they never surrender. Surrender and submission is what gets you through the door into the room of holy communion with the Lord. The blood of Jesus is the contact and access point, but surrender is the pathway.

In that room is where you receive wisdom, guidance, and favor that will carve hours off your day. Instead of laboring from the sweat of your brow in life's daily affairs you will have wisdom and grace to get more accomplished. In that room is where the download of His daily benefits are received. To enjoy the wonderful benefits of Psalm 23, for example, you need to be where the Chief Shepherd is. It's a place in the Spirit that you can access every day.

The blood of Jesus has paved the way for fellowship with God. Through the finished work of Christ these things have already been purchased for you. Legally and positionally we have been blessed with all spiritual blessings in heavenly places in Christ Jesus (Eph 1:3). You are a joint-heir with Christ, but do you know how to access your inheritance? Salvation is free, all by grace, but there is a price to pay to access those places. No man can give you the ability to pay that price. That ability can only come from your own heart.

In that room of blessed communion with the Father is where Jesus moved around in every day and saw what the Father was doing and heard what He was saying. All your fleshly desires die in that room. The love of God transforms you in that room. Your appetites are changed in that room. Strongholds of pride, un-forgiveness, and offense die there. All you thought was important is no longer important in that room. Your prayers are answered in that room because you're praying His will and not your own. And to die daily is your only entrance into that room. You can be satisfied with a low grade of fellowship or you can move up in the Spirit into a higher grade of fellowship with the Trinity.

You have a choice to make each and every day. Will you submit to God's will or your own? If you do refuse Luke 9:23 you can probably still have what many would call a nice life by simply believing the promises of God. The Lord's love for you will not change. And He will come to you again and again and compel you to draw closer to Him. His tender mercies and long-suffering shall be extended to you throughout your entire life in unimaginable ways. You are His child and He will never leave you nor forsake you. But He gives you a choice. Luke 9:23 is a choice.

Will you choose the perfect will of the Lamb who was slain for you? Will you by an act of your own will surrender the ownership of your life to the Lamb and become His bond-slave? This unforced choice is the purest form of love that will make Jesus call you friend (John 15:15). You shall know the sweet, satisfying companionship of the Lord that comes through the fear of the Lord (Pr 25:14) and your unreserved response to His love.

Yes, you can live a nice life without giving the Lord much of yours, but there will be a reckoning both in this life and in eternity when the

Lord shows you what He ordained for you and how short you fell of His perfect will.

Now let me warn you. Here is what will happen when you begin applying Luke 9:23 to your daily walk. You open your Bible and pray. You make several attempts at reviving or increasing your fellowship with God. Your times are dry, and you find it hard to focus. You receive nothing. Your mind and the devil are screaming at you reminding you of all your failures and bringing guilt and condemnation on you. Your mind is being bombarded with thoughts of what you've got to do that day and telling you that you're wasting your time.

The reason these struggles happen frequently with many Christians is because they have not changed realms of operation. They are still in the realm of sense and time. That is, the flesh and the un-harnessed soul still rule. At this point you are faced with a decision. Give up or keep going until you break through into the realm of the Spirit. Ask for more grace. Call on the blood of Jesus. Praying in tongues and fasting will help you immeasurably.

This is a daily process. It will be less and less of a struggle as time goes on. And the time will come when it will not be difficult at all. Your heart will be free and glad. You will rejoice in the Lord as years of weights and strongholds are broken off your life. At times you will actually feel like you are on a spiritual vacation. You will make great advances in the Spirit, but those advances can only be maintained in your daily communion with the Lord.

There are some things we receive from a corporate anointing such as encounters, impartations, and refreshings of the Spirit, but more often than not those blessings are quickly lost if we do not maintain them in our personal communion with God.

Ask yourself: What is sitting on the throne of my heart that I am still trying to find satisfaction and fulfillment from outside of Christ? Who or what is really ruling and governing my life?

I believe one of the final moves of God's Spirit will be to ignite His people with an intense burning passion for God, which will yield true holiness and prepare them for the glory and harvest to come. The purpose of the fire of God is to make us ready for God's glory, to yield the fruit of true holiness in our lives, and to be a glorious Church without spot and wrinkle. This work will only be done in those who submit to God and who are willing to be purged from the desires of the flesh and the world. Luke 9:23 is the way.

# CHAPTER 6

# Rejoicing in the Spirit

*"In that same hour He (Jesus) rejoiced in the Holy Spirit..."* (Lk 10:21a NAS).

What are you rejoicing in? What are you getting excited about? What are you celebrating? When it comes to this subject, there are three categories of people in the church world today: 1) those with little or no rejoicing; 2) those with a false or a natural rejoicing; 3) and those with a pure spiritual rejoicing that is centered on the Lord.

There is a rejoicing in the Spirit we must enter into in this hour. The reason some Christians have little or no rejoicing in their lives is because too many of them are caught up in carnal and temporal things that fade away with time. Too many are living for this world, living as if Jesus will never come, living as if they will never die, and living as if they will never be judged. This is not the posture of a last days' believer. Frankly, this is not Christianity at all.

As long as we are in the world there will be tests and trials, but many people's tests and trials are self-inflicted. When you chase your own happiness, follow your own plan, and put your trust in man you will be disappointed every time. Sorrow shall fill your days, and you will live from crisis to crisis.

We must understand that *the first order of receiving the blessing and enrichment of the Lord in your life is to seek first the kingdom of God and all His righteousness* (Mat 6:33). Without this condition being met you will walk around in circles for the rest of your life and never fulfill God's plan and purpose.

I personally believe that today's churches are full of false converts. They've never been searched out. They've never been convicted of sin. True repentance has never worked in their hearts. They've never made Jesus Lord. There was a well-known preacher who said that in a full gospel church he recently preached in 60% of the couples were living together out of wedlock. And here's the clincher; they didn't know it was wrong!

I have two problems with that. Number one, what was being taught to that church? Number two, why didn't their own hearts condemn them? The answer: I doubt that these people were ever born again. Fornication and adultery are the top physical sins on the catalogue or registry of sins. How can I say that? Because the strength of sin is the law (1 Cor 15:56), and whatever the law says about sin is just how evil that sin is. Sexual immorality is highlighted in the law of God more than any other sin. Those who practice such unrighteousness cannot inherit the kingdom of God (1 Cor 6:9-10; Eph 5:5). The time has come for plain preaching about some of these issues. You can never rejoice in the Spirit while living in sin or in a compromising backslidden state. Many fake it, but the Lord cannot be faked.

The second category of people in our churches today who are not rejoicing in the Spirit are those who are not in a 'first love' position with Jesus, and so their rejoicing is usually limited to some natural or self-motivated thing. It would be interesting to do a church survey about the things that make Christians happy today. I think it would serve as a real eye opener. Some of the answers you might find are: A new and better job offer, or a new and exciting career, the purchase of a home or material things, special honors/awards, money or pay raises/promotions etc. Now again these things can be blessings from the Lord, and we should always be thankful for His provision, but does heaven celebrate these things as much as we often do?

There is a cloud of witnesses surrounding us (Heb 12:1), but it has been said that their concern is mainly for our spiritual affairs. For instance, they don't have great concern of how we are faring in our natural life as much as the spiritual progress we are making. They're not concerned about how much money we have in our bank accounts as much as the spiritual strides we are making in prayer and in our life with God.

Have you noticed that any time angels appeared in the Church age, or visions and supernatural direction was given through prayer, it always had to do with the advancement of the gospel or the salvation and deliverance of people? Now again, there is nothing at all wrong with rejoicing over natural blessings and provision. We need to thank God for every blessing we have, but that is not where our primary focus and rejoicing should be. *Doing the Father's will from a purity of heart produces righteousness, peace, and joy that come from the Holy Ghost.* In other words, a rejoicing in the Lord is manifest in your life from doing the will of God.

Even church leaders can sometimes fall short of a real rejoicing in the Spirit. We can rejoice in ministry opportunities, a new church program, a building program, money, a guest speaker, church attendance etc. None of these things are wrong in themselves if they serve the real purposes of God, but does the Lord celebrate these things as much as we do? That's the issue.

The disciples rejoiced that they had authority over demons (Lk 10), but Jesus channeled their excitement and told them to rejoice in their salvation instead. In other words, rejoice in souls being saved!

*The real rejoicing that Jesus did was when people got their spiritual needs met and the Father's will was done in their lives.*

For most of my life I have felt like a square peg in a round hole. I'm sure when I was younger this was due in part to my own idealism. Some of it however, was due to the integrity of my own heart for the things of God. The "out of place" feelings I've had in different settings and situations over the years were simply a spiritual "disconnection" my spirit would feel to what was going on. At times I just couldn't get excited over the things that others would get excited about. I witnessed too much Hollywood and the spirit of the world in the Church and it always grieved me.

At first I thought there was something wrong with me, but as time went on I realized that the grieving I often felt was coming from the Lord. Hype, showmanship, appearance, and all the professionalism that is often a part of the production of the traditional church culture has never impressed Jesus. What impresses Him is meeting the needs of the heart and real life issues in people's daily struggles. Helping a friend out with monthly rent, paying for a widow's groceries, transporting an invalid person to a church meeting, assisting single parent homes with their children, visiting the sick in hospitals, clothing the naked, visiting those in prison, are some of the things Jesus gets excited about. We are part of a kingdom that places great value on these things. The reason many Christians don't get excited about these things is because these things require a certain amount of personal sacrifice, and therefore are not closely attached to their emotions. Rejoicing in the Spirit does often involve your emotions, but there is an emotional rejoicing that has nothing to do with the Spirit of God.

The Word of God uses the aforementioned acts as the criteria to identify the righteous (Mat 25:31-46) when Jesus comes to set up His earthly Kingdom. What these verses do *not* say is this: Enter into the kingdom the Father has prepared for you because you performed many miracles, cast out many devils, or you prophesied in the Lord's name, had a television ministry, preached to thousands and even millions of people, or you never missed a church service, you sang faithfully in the choir for 30 years, or you went on several mission trips (by the way, there is nothing wrong with most of these acts), or you were prophesied over by a popular TV evangelist, or you received a debt-cancellation prayer cloth with a promise of prosperity. The kingdom we are a part of does not place high value on the sort of acts that are greatly esteemed in much of ministry today.

*There is a part of our Christianity that is very low profile, routine, even a bit mundane, with very little fanfare, always including in our every day affairs opportunities to help and serve others.* Feelings are not always involved, but a quiet confidence and a rejoicing in the Lord will accompany your love and service for others. When you choose to serve the least of all people you are in fact serving Jesus.

I have a prophet friend of mine who received a visitation from Jesus several years ago. He was in a church service located in a red light district where most of its members were former drug addicts, prostitutes, homeless people, and prisoners. *My friend was on his knees worshiping when Jesus said: "I love these kinds of people."*

There's something about Jesus that is so different than natural man. He loves the poor, the broken, and the lowly because they have no pretense and no airs about them. They are real. Jesus found His joy and pleasure in meeting and serving such people. This is where much of His rejoicing was anchored.

Amongst all the hype so prevalent in ministry today, whatever happened to just loving and serving Jesus because He saved you from hell, or just loving Him for who He is? Whatever happened to just simply loving your neighbor as yourself because that's what Jesus said to do?

*There is a great need in the Church today to simplify our lives and our faith, to return to the simplicity of the cross and of loving Jesus and serving others.* Un-plug your emotions from being impressed by big names, big productions, all the professionalism and showmanship of the church enterprise system, and start plugging yourself into the real needs of hurting people around you.

When you start thinking like Jesus and the Father revelation will start flooding your heart. Don't ever be critical of anyone or use your revelation to put others down. Instead, find others of kindred heart and spirit and start looking for opportunities to serve and minister together. Begin thinking of what you have that can bless others. When you do these things you will possess more of the mind of Christ, and you'll find yourself rejoicing in the Spirit as Jesus did.

We're living in the last of the last days. It's a time of great opportunity to touch so many lives. *There are two things I hear the Lord saying:*

1.  Be filled with the Spirit.

2.  Meet the needs of the people.

Keep this as your focus and you will stay right on course, and you'll be ready when Jesus comes.

# CHAPTER 7

# *Consecration*

Back in the 1940's and 1950's there wasn't nearly as much sickness in the Church as there is today. It makes you wonder why. After all, we have much more knowledge and light today in the area of healing than we've ever had before. There are audio and video materials in abundance that deal with this subject. There are many books that have been written concerning our healing covenant and why healing belongs to us. And yet so many in the Church seem to be full of sickness and disease. Why? What's the problem?

A well-known prophet was talking to the Lord about this one time, and the Lord told him that not only were His people healthier years ago, but were much more consecrated, too. There's the answer! *Our consecration is a big part of walking in divine health, and in God's overall plan for our lives.* Sickness and disease is a part of the curse that came with the fall of man. We as Christians have been redeemed from the curse (Gal 3:13). The curse causeless, or without a cause, will not come (Pr 26:2). In other words, the curse cannot come on us without a cause. In the Church age, lack of consecration to God's covenant and plan is the general cause of much sickness.

Think about it. The only reason listed in the scriptures for sickness is found in 1 Cor 11:30—*"For this reason many are weak and sick among you, and many sleep (are dead)."* The reason is listed in the previous verse...*"not discerning the Lord's body."* That has a two-fold application. We must discern the Lord's physical body and His spiritual body. We must discern that the Lord's physical body was broken for our physical health, and we must also discern that the Lord's spiritual body is one and we must walk in love and forgiveness toward every member.

The fruit of the spirit is love (Gal 5:22) and anything contrary to the fruit of the spirit would be under the category of *"the works of the flesh"* (Gal 5:19-21). Even though the Lord will judge a person quicker on spiritual sins or sins of the heart, physical sins will eventually catch up to a believer, too. What do I mean by that?

Love is spiritual. Other sins such as adultery and fornication and the long list in Gal 5:19-21 are physical. Spiritual sins have to do with sins of the heart like unforgiveness, pride, other hidden motives, etc. We cannot judge someone spiritually unless the Lord gives us discernment to see into that realm. We can, however, judge ourselves so that we will not be judged (1 Cor 11:31).

For example, I remember the story of Jack Coe, the great healing evangelist of the 1950's. The Lord sent a prophet, Kenneth Hagin, to warn him of three areas he needed to judge himself on: love, money, and diet. Evangelist Coe wouldn't judge himself so the Lord judged him. He died prematurely at age 38. That was very sad because he had a mighty anointing on him in the healing area. A great ministry was taken from the earth. But the root of Jack Coe's sins was mainly spiritual, things having to do with his love walk and hidden motives of the heart such as pride, jealousy, etc. This is why judgment came quickly.

In contrast, the sin of adultery and fornication are physical sins. Of course they affect our spirits, but for some reason the Lord seems to forbear longer with such sins.

Again, on another occasion, I remember Kenneth Hagin telling a story about a man that finally came under the Lord's judgment after he had lived in adultery for 36 years, never living right for more than two weeks at a time. The man simply wouldn't judge himself, and the Lord eventually had to judge him. And still, amazingly, the Lord had mercy on him when he filled him with the Holy Spirit and blessed him with an extra measure of His presence even in his dying hours. Think about the patience and mercy of God! And yet we also know that such a lifestyle of sin can cause you to lose your good name, reputation, and influence as a Christian, and of course, as a minister. It can also cut your life short and abort God's plan for your life. It never ever pays to sin. Nothing good is ever reaped from sin.

Still the Lord is so merciful and long-suffering with us. Often Christians want to rush to judgment concerning the sins of others. The Lord had already healed this man once even while he was living in adultery. God was demonstrating His goodness so that he would repent, but as I said, he never did live right for more than two weeks at a time. Finally, God's judgment caught up with him and he died.

Why am I sharing all this? Because ministers must teach more on holiness and sanctification. Many in the body of Christ are weak and sickly, and there is another side to healing and experiencing the blessings of

God that is not being taught very much. Disobedience keeps people from getting healed. Disobedience keeps people from receiving God's blessings. Disobedience keeps people from walking in the plan of God. God doesn't bless people so they can continue to live in sin. God doesn't bless people so they can continue to live a selfish lifestyle where they seek their own things and not the things of the kingdom.

Yes, we all sin and miss the mark at times, but it shouldn't be because we want to. *Consecrated people don't sin and miss God because they want to.* The consecrated Christian's aim is to please God in thought, word, motive, and deed. That's the difference. It's a matter of the heart and only God can see the heart. Are you seeking first the kingdom of God (Mat 6:33)?

It is time for our actions and motives to line up with Mat 6:33. There must be a worthy motive in Christians to not only receive healing, but to receive all of God's blessings. If you are sick, why is it that you want to be healed? Why do you want God to deliver you from all your problems and troubles? Why do you desire more monetary and material blessings in your life? Is it only to enjoy your life more, or is it really to serve God? As I said, there is another side of healing that is very rarely taught. In an evangelistic crusade or a healing rally you can't often teach this other side of healing because you are there to get as many people healed as possible in a short time. That is the reason that pastors of local churches need to teach this other side of healing that has to do with our consecration and obedience.

## ANGELS AND OUR CONSECRATION

Lack of consecration can greatly limit angelic ministry to the heirs of salvation. For example, the angels are encamped around about those who *fear* the Lord to keep them in all their ways (Ps 34:7). This scripture is conditional. Walking in the fear of the Lord is the condition believers must meet to ensure angelic protection for their lives.

Not only to angels minister protection, but they are also called to minister provision for the believer. When believers are not consecrated, they move outside of God's path and God's plan for their lives thus hindering the angels from moving on their behalf. Angels will minister very little provision to those who are not endeavoring to follow God's plan for their lives.

We tend to forget about those angels. They are mighty. They excel in strength and hearken to the voice of God's Word (103:20). They are sent by the Lord to minister to us (Heb 1:14), but very often our lack of consecration limits them.

Notice how angels ministered to Jesus after He overcame the temptations of Satan in the wilderness (Mat 4:11). Every time Jesus was tempted He spoke the Word of God. That's what the angels hearken to. But what we fail to often see about these verses is the consecration that Jesus made at the beginning of His earthly ministry. He spent 40 days and nights in prayer and fasting, overcame every temptation the devil threw at Him, and stood His ground, not only against the devil, but against His own flesh and the spirit of the world. The angels then came and ministered to Him.

*Then Jesus said to him, "Be gone, Satan! For it is written, 'You shall worship the Lord your God, and serve Him only.' Then the devil left Him; and behold, <u>angels came and began to minister to Him</u>"* (Mat 4:10-11).

That word 'minister' generally means to do anyone a service and care for someone's needs. Here's something we may not have seen before. Angels are not only committed to the Lord and His Word. They are committed to those who speak His Word and obey it. *In a certain sense angels are drawn to a believer's consecration and their surrender to the Lord's will.*

Notice another example of how angels ministered to Jesus at the end of His ministry in the garden of Gethsemane as Jesus battled to fulfill and complete our redemption. Once again we know what a difficult trial this was for Jesus. In the garden He prayed the same prayer of consecration three times as Matthew records it, and so intense was the struggle that Jesus sweat great drops of blood (Mat 26:44). We see here one more time the correlation between the angels and the consecration Jesus made. Angels honor the word of the Lord and they are activated by a believer's consecration and surrender.

**"Now an angel from heaven appeared to Him, strengthening Him" (Luke 22:43).**

Not only do angels minister protection and strength to us, but they minister preparation and provision for us also in many different areas. A minister received the following vision from the Lord that wonderfully illustrates this and agrees with scripture.

The vision was about a young mother with two small children whose husband had left her. At this time she was without a job, her car was broke down, she had no money to provide day care for her children, and she was living with her parents and complaining to the Lord about the lack of provision in her life. The Lord then showed this minister two pathways into this woman's future symbolized by two assembly lines. The first pathway was all lit up and showed angels darting in and out while others stood on the side arranging things. This represented the perfect will of God for her life for the next two years. All the provision the woman had been praying for and needed had already been commanded by the Lord and prepared by the angels.

The other pathway was not lit up very well and there were only one or two angels on it looking rather inactive. This was the path the woman was currently on which was outside the will of God.

The woman was facing some decisions in her life that required growth and character and a stronger consecration and obedience from her. But she was emotionally unwilling to surrender and do what was right. She was looking for answers but in the wrong place. For example, she was in her parents' church instead of another church that the Lord was leading her to. In that other church God had commanded three different people to bless this woman. One was to fix her car, one was to give her a job as a receptionist, and the other was to babysit her children. All this provision had been prepared by the angels for her to walk in, but due to her disobedience she was not receiving it.

Remember the story of Elijah and the widow of Zarephath (1 Kings 17:8-16). The Lord had commanded this widow to sustain Elijah, but when he arrived there the lady was preparing what she thought was her last meal, unaware that a miraculous provision had been commanded from heaven. Both her obedience and Elijah's obedience to the word of the Lord manifested the provision.

Angels are sent by the Lord to make preparations for our provision, but we've got to stay consecrated to the will and the plan of God to receive it. Angels have no authority to change God's plans nor to give people slack or forgive their disobedience. They are simply sent to do a job and they have no emotional attachment to people.

When my family and I moved from Pensacola, Florida to New England in late summer of 2006 I was conscious of the Lord's timing and provision. Our house in Pensacola had been on the market for a number of months and hardly anyone was even looking at it, much less interested in purchasing it. Suddenly the second person that viewed the home purchased it, and we made a trip to New England and found a new home to purchase there within 3 days. Things had been so slow to develop up until that point, but then they happened so quickly.

I'm convinced that the angels had a definite timetable they were working with. We wanted to be in New England by the spring but the angels had prepared for late summer. It didn't matter how much we spoke the Word or believed God for our home to sell at a certain time. The angels have no liberty to change God's plans or timetable. Often we push things and try to force something to happen outside of the timing of the Lord. Part of our consecration is not only to God's plans but His timing also. We've got to learn to follow our hearts and not our heads.

I could list a number of other examples from my own personal life where my obedience accelerated provision and where my disobedience to God's plans or timing caused delays. Let's judge ourselves in these areas of consecration. Are you walking in love with other members in the body of Christ? How about with your spouse and children, and relatives? Is there any un-forgiveness in your heart toward anyone? Do you want others to succeed as much as you want to succeed? Are you free of pride and selfish motives? Why do you want God's blessings? Why do you want financial peace and independence? Are your motives worthy of God's favor? Are you consecrated to the will and plan of God for your life whatever that may be? Are things in order in your heart?

# CHAPTER 8

# The Martyr Heart

*"But this I say, brethren, the time is short, so that from now on even those who have wives should be as though they had none, those who weep as though they did not weep, those who rejoice as though they did not rejoice, those who buy as though they did not possess, and those who use this world as not misusing it. For the form of this world is passing away)...But I want you to be without care...that you may serve the Lord without distraction"* (1 Cor 7:29-32, 35).

The Spirit Filled Life Bible has these comments to make concerning the above passage:

*"Paul presents this teaching in light of the tension between the temporal, unredeemed, secular order and the believer's spiritual life and calling. The present distress applies to the whole of this age and not to some distinct period of persecution in the first century. The spirit of this entire age is stressful, temporal, and distracting.*

*Because of the nature of this age and the reality of the coming of Christ, believers are to adopt the attitude of finding the source of their life in*

*Christ, rather than in earthly institutions, whether marriage, the social sphere, or the economic world. A Christian is to live intently and responsibly and yet see these realities as ultimately temporal."*

This entire theme speaks of living unsettled, not putting down your roots in this temporal place called earth, and living as spiritual pilgrims passing through. Whether you live here in the comforts of America or in some impoverished underdeveloped nation, or somewhere inbetween, you can live in a state of unsettledness.

Let me illustrate with a couple of personal examples what it means to live in this attitude.

A pastor friend of mine whom I will call Bill, a family man and nearly 50 at the time, sat with me at lunch one day and shared some deep thoughts and feelings he was experiencing. Tired of a lack of fruit-bearing power among some of his long-standing church members, and all the fluff that goes with the profession of conventional ministry, he spoke of leaving his established church of some 20 years and living a different sort of Christianity. He spoke of selling his home, too and totally unhooking from the familiar past that he had known. "I scare my wife every time I talk this way." He said.

"What will you do?" I asked. I'll get a regular job, gather me a band of radical disciples like Jesus did, win souls, and live out authentic relationship-based New Testament Christianity.

What would make Bill leave a fairly successful small community church with all its security, comforts, and benefits that took him years to build up, and just leave it all?

Let me take you through more of the conversation and you'll see. Please realize that I'm only using this one man's experience to prove a point.

He told me in so many words that he was tired of professional Christianity, fearing the Church, as he knew it, was becoming a bit of a dinosaur, irrelevant in many ways, and not connecting the dots between theory and what they actually possessed in reality.

Bill shared with me how disappointed he was recently when a long standing member of his church, a licensed practical nurse by profession, failed to share the gospel with a dying man, leading the poor man to believe that there was somehow hope outside of Christ: "I hope he finds a better place when he dies." the nurse lamented.

The pastor was flabbergasted when he heard this! After years of sermons, teaching and training, all this church member had was theory— teachings she had yet to learn to apply in real life.

Bill shared other examples of this same type of spiritual dysfunction in his church. Not that there weren't any serious students of the Word, but there were far too many who displayed a sharp indifference between what they heard and what they actually made work in the real world. Bill's longing was to develop disciples in the real world, outside of the traditional setting of the organized church. In other words, his passion was to make disciples in life relationships, which he felt might be more effective, as opposed to the more traditional and structured way of doing it.

Please understand that it doesn't really matter what model or methods you use to make true disciples, as long as it is effective. I'm sharing a personal example to show you how much Bill, a long time pastor with an established church, was willing to give up in order to follow the Lord's direction for his life and live like the pilgrim that he was called to be.

Actually the more I listened to Pastor Bill talk the more I could identify with him. The babe leaped in my own womb as I realized more and more that true disciples of Jesus Christ have zero tolerance for complacency, indifference, and are quickly bored with the status quo. My own heart bore witness with Bill's convictions and I sensed God being drawn into our conversation.

*True disciples of Jesus have a martyr's heart.*

I know of another brother, a former student of mine, now an evangelist who travels to unreached regions where few men will dare to go. I e-mailed him to ask about the cost of a 5-country preaching tour he was currently on. In a reply communiqué he writes:

*"Good hearing from you. I hope all is well there in the States. Better you than me. I have no family, no home, no personal belongings, and of course, no payments.*

*If you don't mind going low budget like me you can do the trip for reasonably cheap. Once you get to Bangkok (BKK) the flights are less than you would expect if you go on a budget airliner. The risk of going into immediate glory can run a little higher. If you want to run to win then it's not a problem. Crash landings are sure to get you there before the rest of the pack.*

*I should be in the States for about 3 months if the Lord tarries. I want to drop the hammer while I'm there. I might not ever get another chance to preach in the ole USA again. I'm surprised we're still hanging in there.*

*Like I said, time is short. Who knows what will happen between now and then? All hell is about to break loose! The restrainer is about to be removed!"*

These are the words of what I call a martyr heart. At this writing this brother was nearly 40 years of age and has chosen to live unmarried and unhooked from earthly possessions to serve Jesus whole-heartedly. He constantly speaks of his love for the lost masses of unreached people groups who have not yet heard the true gospel. Not everyone is called to be a missionary and live this way, but everyone is called to be a disciple of Jesus and live with the same mind-set and attitude (Mat 10:37-39; 16:24-25) (Lk 14:33) in whatever sphere of life they are in.

Some may find the above examples a bit excessive and say, "I'm not a full time minister. I have a family to support, and bills to pay. There is no way I can live like this." In the above opening passage of scripture the point Paul is making is to live without cares and distractions, unhooked from the temporal things of this world, still being responsible, but finding your total source of life in Christ. You can do this in any line of work or field of study. The main point is to live as if this world is not your final destination. Just think: If you die tomorrow, what of all your earthly endeavors?

*Why don't you die today while still in the body?*

That is the martyr heart. In other words, you are dead to the things of this world and you are living solely for eternity. This is the attitude that attracts the presence of Jesus.

Think of what you find attractive or appealing in other human beings. Perhaps it is a kindness or a respect they show for other people. Maybe it is a humble and yielded disposition they possess that attracts you. The spirit of humility is always attractive for God Himself is drawn to a humble heart (Jam 4:6). But the greatest and most appealing quality in any human being is the love and compassion of God. And it is this love and compassion that moves a martyr's heart and makes him irresistible.

I recently read the story of Angelo. Angelo was a homeless man, who after being saved, laid down his life for other homeless people. His earthly life came to an end when he died on top of another homeless man in the dead of winter trying to keep him warm. Even though Angelo was a virtual unknown to the world, his reward in heaven is great. He died a martyr.

*This is why a martyr's heart draws and attracts the presence of Jesus like nothing else can.*

Notice how Jesus stood up at the right hand of God to behold the persecution of Stephen (Acts 7:55), and then receive him into glory. Isn't that amazing? A martyr's heart is irresistible to Jesus. There is an incredible earthward pull from heaven into the martyr heart. Angels marvel at the faith of a martyr and minister to them in their hour of temptation and need (Mat 4:11).

Martyrdom is a manifestation of the fullness of true covenant. This is what it means to eat His flesh, drink His blood (John 6:53-56), and be a close friend to Jesus. It's all about laying down your life in a spirit of pure love. You see, the scriptures do warn us that it is possible to make sacrifices and even be a physical martyr without love (1 Cor 13:1-3). Suicide bombers are a good modern day example of this.

Laying down one's life for the glory of God to the point of physical death is truly the supreme act that embodies the fullness of martyrdom. Yet any serious believer can demonstrate a martyr's heart every day by the life they choose to live. The kingdom of God needs living martyrs, too.

*When heaven becomes more real than this world the martyr heart is conceived.*

The early apostles died martyrs because they were not attached to this world or afraid of leaving it. The post-resurrection appearances of Jesus had stamped eternity in their hearts. When some of them witnessed Jesus lifting up His hands and blessing them, and then disappearing into the sky and on into the third heaven (Lk 24:50-53), they could not contain themselves. Worship, joy, and praise erupted from their hearts, and earthly things lost a permanent grip on their lives.

Stephen was the Church's first martyr. He was a young man in the prime of his life and probably had a family. He chose to preach an uncompromising message one day, and never returned to his earthly home, choosing instead to move on to his eternal home. What is inside of the heart of a man like that? What would make a young man seal his fiery message with his own blood?

I believe Stephen was drunk with a spirit of martyrdom. I believe that the Holy Spirit so filled him with visions of heaven and glory that pushed Stephen over the edge and on into the presence of the Lord. There was a grace from God released for Stephen to die a martyr's death.

Stephen was a holy vessel of a wholly new order effecting disorder among the self-righteous crowd. He was fit for the Master's use but so unfit for the religious system of his day. God raised him up in a blaze of great persecution. Stephen answered the call, and never looked back. Jesus was alive and heaven was real. Earth's sights vanished and its sounds were silenced as Stephen's spirit left his bruised and battered body and ascended upward.

I often wonder: Will there be end time persecution in America as great as that which was in Jerusalem long ago? And will there again be Stephens among us who have grandeur visions of heaven and of the glory of God? And will some be killed for telling the truth?

*A martyr heart sets things in motion for other generations.*

We have reason to believe that Stephen's forgiveness of his accusers and murderers was instrumental in bringing forth new birth in another young man named Saul. As Stephen's life on earth ended with visions of heaven, Saul's new life would soon begin with the same. And as Stephen suffered this great persecution so Saul would suffer much more.

Saul became Paul because Stephen cried for his forgiveness. The witnesses at his death laid down their clothes at Saul's feet. But it was Stephen's loud praying that would later lay down new paths for those same feet.

Stephen's violent departure led to Saul's violent entry into the kingdom of God. Will an increase of this kind of violence mark the last days? Will there be an increase in the voices of violent praying, preaching, and forgiveness that will produce more violent conversions in this generation?

*A true martyr heart is abandoned to Jesus. A false martyr heart is not.*

Think about this: Many without Christ possess this kind of spirit. Many die willingly for unrighteous causes. Some inner city gangs could be considered fearless martyrs. In many ways they live a life of complete abandonment. The same could be said of Islamic terrorists.

But their martyrdom is born out of hate, desperation, and anger. When they die they leave one hell and enter another. There are no grandeur visions of heaven and of the glory of God. How tragic! And yet how tragic also when you compare today's hell martyr spirit versus our own. They are sadly deceived, but we know the truth. Do we love our own lives more than they do? Are they more devoted to a lie that we are the truth?

There's a new generation called "Y" who dress in vampire garb and have an obsession with death and darkness. They too are not afraid to die. Their perverted identity with death has conquered their fear of it. They've made Satan their friend. Isn't it interesting how they've landed on a scriptural principle? Generation "Y" hates their natural life, and that's why they are willing and able to give themselves to Satan's kingdom. What an eerie perversion and morbid corruption of such a great spiritual truth!

Think of someone like Evel Knievel, the stunt cyclist. If he doesn't have a spirit of martyrdom and wreckless abandonment, I don't know who does. Yet he does it for fun and a strange brand of entertainment. Getting on a motorcycle and riding as fast as he can, he endeavors to jump it over 27 automobiles. Flying through the air before gathered thousands, see Evel land successfully but not safely on the other side. The motorcycle tumbles and Evel rolls, breaking many bones in his body. I believe anyone who would do that at the risk of his own life is drunk with another spirit. In Evel's case, it may be a strange spirit, but in Stephen's case it was the Holy Spirit.

The Holy Spirit will always lead us to lose our lives in utter abandonment for Christ's sake. Losing your life for Jesus' sake will cause you to gain it!

That is the martyr heart.

# CHAPTER 9

# *Eternity in the Heart: The Spirit of Evangelism*

Heaven or hell…heaven or hell…heaven or hell…One hundred years from now where will we all be? If it's heaven, what will be your standing? What will be your eternal reward? What will be your eternal position with Jesus? Will you reap of gold, silver, and precious stones or will your works go up in smoke as wood, hay, and stubble? (1 Cor 3:12-15)

And what of your family, friends, and neighbors? And what of all the lost people you know? Where will they be? Oh God, there's such inspiration in my belly for the fulfillment of the great commission and a reaping of the precious fruit of the earth that remains!

*"For I am full of words; the spirit within me compels me. Indeed my belly is like wine that has no vent; it is ready to burst like new wineskins. I will speak, that I may find relief; I must open my lips and answer"* (**Job 32:18-20**).

*"For we cannot but speak the things which we have seen and heard"* (**Acts 4:20**).

Let me speak to you as an evangelist. The true work of evangelism is one of the most neglected in the Church, and yet it is one of the most important. I'm not even sure that many of us understand this ministry. Contrary to popular thought and opinion, evangelism is not just the announcement of the good news of the gospel, but it is also a call to warn people of the judgment to come as the apostle Paul did before Felix the governor.

*"Some days later Felix came with his wife Drusilla who was a Jewess; and he sent for Paul and listened to him talk about <u>faith in Christ Jesus</u>. But as he continued to <u>argue</u> about uprightness, purity of life, the control of the passions (temperance or self-control), and <u>the judgment to come</u>, Felix became <u>alarmed and terrified</u> and said, Go away for the present; when I have a convenient opportunity I will send for you"* (Acts 24:24-25 Amp).

Paul did not hold back. He warned the governor of the eternal consequences of living in sin. The above verses tell us that these themes of righteousness, self-control, and of the judgment to come that Paul expounded on were all part of the faith in Christ Jesus, and of the gospel he preached. I'm not so sure we understand that this is all a part of the gospel. People must know they are sick before they can appreciate and receive the cure. Sin is sickness, and Christ is the cure. Paul didn't just preach the cure, he preached about the sickness too.

Notice also how Paul "argued" and spoke passionately, something we need much more of today. Sometimes we can be such a passion-less people, but Paul was a man of overwhelming passion.

*"Now while Paul was awaiting them at Athens, <u>his spirit was grieved and roused to anger</u> as he saw the city was full of idols, <u>so he reasoned and argued</u> in the synagogue..."* (Acts 17:16-17 Amp).

*"By the time Silas and Timothy arrived from Macedonia, Paul was <u>completely engrossed</u> with preaching, earnestly <u>arguing and testifying</u> to the Jews that Jesus is the Christ"* (Acts 18:5 Amp).

I've been in that place in the spirit so many times over the years. I've had people tell me to tone things down, to not get too excited, to not raise my voice so loud, but they just didn't understand the passion of one who knows, as a messenger of God, he stands between the living and the dead. A dying preacher once said, *"I've taken a good look into eternity, and if I could come back, how different I would preach."*

If we're not careful, our preaching can become heady, but heart-less, informative but passion-less. It can lack revelation of the otherworld and the life to come. Desperate times require desperate preaching. The urgency of the hour requires an urgent message. When a house is on fire and its inhabitants are perishing, an urgent response is demanded. And so, will we not help those whose souls are on the edge of the fire of hell?

Paul's spirit was *"grieved and roused to anger; he reasoned, argued, testified, and was completely engrossed with preaching."* This beloved man was possessed with another spirit. God gripped him. The words he penned throughout his epistles are full of strong emotions and consuming passions that still vibrate in the hearts of those who are also consumed with eternity.

The words that Paul spoke to Felix alarmed and terrified him. Somehow we've come to believe that words, which soothe and comfort are the only words we need to be speaking. How grave a mistake that is! How many have perished because there was no voice of inspiration that to arouse them from their slumber? We must speak to the lost as if it were our last opportunity, with tenderness, love, and passion dripping from our lips, and weeping, if possible, through every argument. We must learn the art and skill of compelling sinners to Christ.

When I visit churches I see such a need for the impartation of the zeal and fire of evangelism. I see such a need for the ministry of the evangelist and for the local church to share its resources and to support worthy men who fill that ministry.

It's so easy for the local church and its officers to become complacent and to take on a form of academia and ecclesiasticism that kills the spirit of revival and the zeal for evangelism. There has been a great deal of secularization in so many of our congregations across America and the world.

Listen to the words of Gordon Lindsay:

*"The tendency of the paid clergy in general has been to ecclesiasticism, the development of a form of religion and the freezing of it into a static condition. An office in the church can be made into a professional thing, a means of making a living. A man caught in the toils of its vicious cycle is to be pitied. God calls every minister to be a guardian of the souls of men."*

We need to take the gospel out of the secularization state and out of the academic sphere and apply it to the individual in terms of life and death and heaven and hell. Let's put the gospel into the personal realm of human experience. The ministry of evangelism reminds men that beyond this world there is an after-life, and all of humanity is but one heart-beat away from eternity; to either enter heaven, the abode of the righteous, or hell, the regions of the damned…forever!

All the forces of evil are arrayed against the gospel penetrating the minds and hearts of sinners. The devil's strategy has always been to institutionalize the Church and to turn it into a powerless religious system where it has little consciousness of eternity and no zeal for the conversion of lost souls. If the devil can turn the Church into a business that deals mainly with the dollar in mind, or into a charitable organization that is satisfied with humanitarian projects only, or into a social club or an entertainment center, he has succeeded, and he will rear his proud head back with glee for doing so. *The Church has been ordained by God to be above all else, a soul-saving organism.*

The devil will use division from within the church and persecution from without the church to stop the gospel from spreading. It is obvious from reading through the gospels and the book of Acts that there were revivals, but there were also riots and fierce opposition to the gospel, to the work of evangelism, and the conversion of sinners. Satan will use every strategy in his arsenal to keep Christians from preaching the gospel and to keep sinners from receiving it.

As an example of the latter, I was on the streets one time helping a local church with evangelistic outreach when my team and I were invited into a home. As soon as I began to bear down and preach the gospel to some of the members of that household, distractions began to come. I would say the word 'hell' and the landline phone would ring. I would say the name of Jesus and how foolish it was to live without God and the cell phone would ring. Conviction would come and someone would knock on the door or start playing with the dog. When the opportunity to receive Jesus was given, the conversation would move into a natural direction as the devil toyed with people's minds.

I decided to tell the people what was happening, thus exposing the devil's devices. That must have shut him up for good because suddenly all the distractions ceased and the presence of God moved in, and you couldn't hear a pin drop for the next 30 minutes as the people, out of a willing heart, called on the name of the Lord with joy and tears. It was glorious! My team and I didn't want to engage in any casual conversation after we left the house because of the richness of the presence and the peace of God we had just experienced.

What an impression this made on the sinners who were saved! They didn't just utter a prayer or make a confession, but they received an impartation. The two members of my team were also deeply impacted. These are the kind of experiences that will make soul winners out of common men. You can't get this from a textbook. It is not the enticing words of man's speech but it is the impartation that comes through demonstrations of the Holy Spirit that will eternally and permanently leave its mark on people.

In the light of eternity what are the things in this life that really matter? In comparison to the eternal destiny of the human race, how insignificant are so many of life's trivialities! There is nothing we can take with us to heaven except people. Jesus' final message to His disciples still rings true, and all the more as we see the day of His return approaching: *"He that believes and is baptized shall be saved and he that believes not shall be damned"* (Mk 16:15-16).

May the damned be less.

And may the Lord saturate us with an undying zeal for the souls of men.

CHAPTER 10

# *Evangelize or Die*

Many centuries ago in North Africa there was a strong Christian movement and presence throughout the region. Today Islam rules and in some nations Islamic governments have instituted laws that make preaching and converting men to Christ a criminal offense. What happened? How could nations and regions that were once Christianized become such strongholds of Islam?

History tells us the story. In North Africa when Christian theologians began to have doctrinal disagreements the emphasis on the great commission was diminished, and then the devil gradually moved in.

*"Go into all the world and preach the gospel to every creature...he who believes and is baptized shall be saved...and these signs shall follow those who believe"* **(Mk 16:15).** These final words of Jesus are so powerful, and yet so easy to neglect and lose sight of. Simply put, the Church is commanded to evangelize with signs following, or reap the consequences. The consequences in North Africa for not keeping the great commission, as the Church's central focus, were death to the

move of God and Christianity. Think of the many generations that have been affected by the Church's neglect in North Africa. The same I'm sure could be said of many other nations.

Europe is another continent that was entrusted with the gospel in the early centuries and at one time had many strong churches that dotted its landscape. Yet today, a good number of the European nations are like sewers infested with atheism, humanism, and false religion. Neglecting to focus on the fulfillment of the great commission with power allowed darkness to move in.

The same could be said of local churches everywhere: Lutheran churches; Methodist churches; Presbyterian churches; Pentecostal churches; Charismatic churches. In their earliest beginnings many of these churches experienced revival and were zealous in evangelistic work. Many have since grown cold and complacent and some have died.

Several years ago a friend of mine ministered in a church with approximately 60–70 people. The Spirit of God gave him three words to preach on. "Evangelize or die!" Some people were angry and offended at this word. The church, however, soon got past being offended and entered into obedience. In a very short time this church grew to 700 people. "Evangelize or die" is an in season word for many churches today. Just imagine what would happen to the body of Christ worldwide if this word was taken seriously.

Here is what I've observed in local churches: Man-hours, energy, focus, money, time, and resources are put into different areas of the church, but evangelistic work is sorely neglected. Oh yes, we have our outreach programs, but many of these are service or socially oriented works only. The zeal of God and the real soul-winning spirit can sometimes be lacking. We need fresh fire! We need a touch of wholesome fanaticism!

Evangelism is the purpose, and we need to keep the purpose at the forefront. Service is good, but service with evangelism is far better. The purpose is to get people saved by preaching the gospel with signs following (Mk 16). We are commanded to do good works and service-oriented programs are certainly a part of that, but in and of itself, these programs cannot save anyone.

Listen to this powerful statement:

*"There is a certain kind of passivity, a teaching and an educating to bring truth and an engaging in acts of kindness to show love, that actually limits the ministry of God's kingdom."*

Without question, we must continue to teach and educate people with truth and demonstrate the love of God, especially through acts of service and kindness, but without a certain kind of zeal and a preaching with power, the kingdom of God makes very little penetration into the world.

The Salvation Army organization is an example of what has happened in many Christian churches and institutions when service and social programs are placed above the fervent preaching of the gospel. Many of our Salvation Army centers today are social organizations only, with little or no fire (how many times has a Salvation Army worker shared Christ with you especially during holidays like Christmas when donations are received outside department stores and supermarkets?).

William Booth, the founder of the Salvation Army, was not only a compassionate man who loved and served the poor, and was rich in good works, but he was also a man full of fire, vision, and passion. It was General Booth who made the following statement more than 100 years ago:

*"The chief danger of the 20th century will be religion without the Holy Ghost, Christianity without Christ, forgiveness without repentance, salvation without regeneration, heaven without hell, and politics without God."*

What a word of wisdom! How accurate and fitting is this utterance for the present hour generation! Even his own organization has for the most part fallen prey to this amazing prophecy.

We must realize that God has chosen the foolishness of preaching to save those who believe (1 Cor 1:17-18, 21). Do we really understand that without preaching people cannot be saved? The early apostles serve as our timeless examples that public preaching is necessary to the growth of the Church. But the task of preaching the gospel wasn't committed only to the apostles. Everyone preached the gospel in the early Church.

*"Therefore they that were scattered abroad went everywhere preaching the word"* (Acts 8:4).

*"Now they which were scattered abroad upon the persecution that arose about Stephen traveled as far as Phenice, and Cyprus, and Antioch, preaching the word…And some of them were men of Cyprus and Cyrene, which, when they were come to Antioch, spake unto the Grecians, preaching the Lord Jesus"* (Acts 11:19-20).

Now think about this: The early Church preached the gospel during times of great persecution. How much easier it is to preach during times of relative peace? When the Church fails to preach the gospel during times of peace, evil advances. The devil is merciless. Haven't we seen this in America where courts are assuming more power than any branch of our federal government and seeking to uphold laws that would limit the preaching of the gospel? Even now it is happening! This is not the time to back down. This is the time for the Church to step up her efforts in prayer and the public preaching of the gospel with signs following.

What happens when unfavorable laws toward the preaching of the gospel begin to be legislated? The intimidation factor increases. It then becomes easier to keep silent or to compromise our message. Scripture commands us to obey the laws of the land, but not when they are contrary to the laws of God. The principle is that we always submit to the higher law. "Preaching the gospel to every creature" (Mk 16:15) is the higher law.

Richard Wurmbrand, founder of Voice of the Martyrs, who suffered much for the gospel, once asked why, when the Supreme Court passed the law removing public prayer from our schools, American Christians complied. What would have happened if we just refused to comply and say like Peter and the other apostles, **"We ought to obey God rather than men (Acts 5:29)?"** That ungodly law might have been reversed immediately. Or at the least, the Church would've proven by her obedience to be a force to be reckoned with. By not taking action and being silent we allowed darkness to move in and increase.

This is how the devil moved into North Africa. First, the Church became divided over doctrine and gradually grew spiritually cold.

Then things began to decline from there…they stopped praying, they stopped evangelizing, they became ashamed of the gospel and kept it in a closet, public preaching decreased, and eventually became non-existent. And then Satan pounced on the opportunity, and increased his efforts to make the preaching of the gospel illegal.

In the process of time new laws were passed by anti-Christ governments that restricted the Christian witness. Principalities and powers began to rule the land. Today in that region you can feel the fear and oppression that Islam has produced. Now the only way to advance the gospel in much of that region is to work 'underground' or pay the ultimate price of martyrdom.

When the early Church and the apostles received persecution they kept on preaching. (Acts 4:18-20) (Acts 5:28-29, 40-42). It's about time we do the same.

Evangelize or die! Every saint is called to be a witness. The honorable task of evangelizing our world does not fall on a chosen few. It is to be a lifestyle. It should not be relegated to a special department in the church. Otherwise, people get the impression that evangelistic work is only for a chosen and tireless few, and it compartmentalizes the purpose of evangelism instead of enlarging it.

Just imagine if every Christ-professing church, evangelical, denominational, or otherwise really preached the gospel! What a difference we would see in our own nation and in the nations of the world!

Where is the problem? Why is there so little zeal for evangelism in many of our churches? Why is the harvest so great and the laborers still so few? It is because to most Christians evangelism is a law and a duty. But evangelism is only a law and a duty to those who still own their lives. Until you yield your life to the ownership of Jesus Christ, evangelism will continue to be drudgery to you. People will be a sort of 'project' for you to invite to church, and the love and compassion of Jesus that breaks the enemy's back and fuels evangelism will be lacking. Falling in love with Jesus will change all that. If you love Jesus with all your heart you will share Him with your life and with your mouth.

*"A burning heart will find for itself a flaming tongue."* Charles Spurgeon

Much of our evangelistic activity can be done in vain if believers are not experiencing the presence of God that comes from living a submitted life to Jesus.

Here is what real Christians must do: Allow yourself to be broken before the Lord. Don't just spend time in prayer, but also spend time in surrender. Submit to His Lordship daily (Lk 9:23). At first it will be a battle in your soul, but if you stay with it, every action of your life will soon start becoming an act of worship and every person a target of God's love. You will be transformed!

The culmination of this transformation in you will be evidenced in your thoughts. You will begin to find yourself thinking about God and thinking about people in the light of His redemption. Your feelings will also change. You will begin to feel God's heart for people and to pray His desires.

The living Church of the Lord Jesus Christ is the only hope for our world. As the Church goes, so goes the nation. But the Church is only as powerful as its commitment to pray and live a surrendered life, and be obedient to the great commission. When churches fail to obey the great commission and go public with the gospel you will find the Holy Spirit's influence gradually being removed. "Evangelize or die" is an urgent word. I believe obedience to this word will revive churches and rescue the perishing multitudes.

# CHAPTER 11

# Heaven, Hell, and Holiness

I want to speak about the three BIG H'S: Heaven, Hell, and Holiness. I call these forgotten themes or lost themes in the body of Christ. If preachers would begin to preach about heaven many people would be glad to hear about it, but not so many would have the same feelings toward hell. *But did you know that Jesus, our loving and merciful Savior, gave more actual descriptions of hell than He did of heaven?*

Listen to a voice from the Puritan past:

*"Oh! If we had more love to you, we would tell you more about hell. They do not love you who do not warn you, poor hell-deserving sinners. Oh! Remember that love warns."*

Jesus said that hell is a real place "where their worm does not die and the fire is not quenched" (Mk 9:44). He also describes it as a furnace of fire where there is wailing, weeping, and gnashing of teeth (Mat 13:50), and a place of continual torment (Lk 16:23-24). Only those whose names are in the Lamb's Book of Life will enter heaven (Rev 21:27) while those not found therein will be thrown into the lake of fire

(Rev 20:15). Not too popular, but Jesus and the holy Scriptures give it plenty of attention.

In His oft-proclaimed warnings of hell Jesus spoke of death and the judgment to come as well. And the frequency by which He spoke of these things agrees with the pattern of the entire New Testament. Actually, there are 234 references of death, hell, and judgment in 260 chapters of the NT. Isn't it disturbing that so few preachers today preach on these vitally important themes? We've practically taken them out of the gospel. I did a study on hell a couple of years ago and learned so much. It made me even more grateful for my salvation, and it nurtured a greater compassion and burden in me for the lost.

*We must understand that the great purpose of divine revelation is to warn men that their eternal destiny is permanently determined by the manner which they live their earthly life.* Therefore that which determines man's destiny in the next life should have man's most reverent attention in this one. Today many Christians are only interested in this life. There seems to be so very little talk about the afterlife. Frankly, many act as if their lives on earth will never end.

There is a real need in the Church today to restore the preaching of these truths to our theology. The fact that they are emphasized in the New Testament means the Church should emphasize them. One of the most convicting and alarming truths known to man is that he must someday meet God. Barring the return of Jesus, every man will one day die, and every man will one day be judged.

Yet the apostle Paul said he couldn't wait for that day, desiring to depart from this world, and calling it *"far better"* to do so than to stay (Phil 1:23). Why then are so many Christians afraid or hesitant to talk about these things? And why are preachers reluctant to preach on them? The lost must be told of heaven and warned of hell and judgment. The saved must be encouraged to live holy and press on toward their eternal reward, knowing that what they do after their salvation will determine their rank, position, and reward in heaven throughout all eternity.

*Are we so bound to our earthly home, forgetting we're just passing through, that the reality of our eternal home has totally faded from our view?*

Even though Jesus did not talk much about heaven in the way of description, there are several places in the Bible where heaven or paradise and the New Jerusalem are mentioned. This is our blessed hope!

Heaven is the home of the redeemed. Jesus said He went away to prepare 'dwelling places' for us (John 14:2-3). Yes, literal homes! And do you know what those homes will be made out of? Gold, silver, and precious stones which represent our works tried by fire (1 Cor 3:12-13)! And do you know what the greatest part of the judgment of our works is based on? Our motives and whether our works were based on pure love and for the glory of God (See my Purity of Heart book).

In Revelation 21 when the angel showed John the New Jerusalem, the Bride of Christ (that's the consecrated and surrendered people of God), some of the construction of the city had been finished. The wall and its foundations were named after the apostles. That is to say, the construction materials of gold, silver, and precious stones to furnish this part of the holy city were supplied from the consecrated lives of the apostles. The apostles suffered great persecution and martyrdom to take the Lord's love to the nations. Their motives purified their works, and their works were translated into materials to help construct the foundations of the wall of the New Jerusalem. Glory to God!

Just think: *Every trial, every difficulty, every sacrifice you've made, every word and deed you've done in love and for the honor and glory of God is being translated into construction materials to furnish your heavenly home.* Even the heavenly clothing of the saints will be furnished from their righteous acts (Rev 19:8). That is so incredible to me! That is such a motivating factor to keep on pressing toward the mark for the prize of the high calling that's in Christ Jesus! Our goal, though, must be like the apostle Paul's, to know Him (Phil 3:10). We do not necessarily serve the Lord for the rewards only, but out of a passion and love for Him who first loved us (1 John 4:19).

All that is done with pure motives will get the Lord's reward. When your motives are pure your love is pure. That is true holiness. Pure love is holiness. And pure love will not be ashamed in the day when His holy fire will test our works.

Holiness is not a popular message today. One of the reasons it's not popular is because of the misconception people have of holiness. Many still equate holiness with rules and restrictions. But living holy is not about what you wear and how you dress, or about the length of your hair, or even the outward blessings you may have. Holiness is the character of God. It's the nature and love of God.

*Jesus was the perfect example of holiness. He was holy because he was ruled by love in all things.* Every thought, word, and deed he ever did was motivated by love. Every act of His life was a contribution to the glory of God. Even the miracles He performed were not so much to prove His own deity, but out of a love and compassion for humanity. How wonderful and burden destroying is His love!

Understand that Jesus did not preach the gospel and heal the sick because He was trying to earn points from the Father. He didn't lay down

His life and forgive His enemies so He could earn wages from the Father and make it back to heaven. He never did anything for money, popularity, or to gain a name or an advantage for Himself. Simply put, everything Jesus said and did was out of love and for the glory of God alone regardless of public opinion. That, my friends, is holiness!

Have you ever met someone you knew who was hiding something and not telling you the truth? Hiding is a manifestation of sin and pride. The first thing Adam and Eve did when they sinned in the beginning was to hide. This is just the opposite of holiness. *Holiness has an unveiled and open face.* It doesn't hide because it has nothing to hide. In the day of reckoning and accountability and the revealing of all things, nothing can be hidden from the fire of His holiness.

Pride hides. Holiness is transparent. *The more transparent a person is the greater holiness he is walking in.* When people have ulterior motives and a certain self-seeking agenda, they will twist their words or an event to their own advantage; they will use people for their own gain, courting words to their own favor, often shading the truth to put themselves in the best possible light and to protect themselves. Almost every human being has something they hide. The only ones who don't are the Father, the Son, and the Holy Spirit. Our goal should always be the image of Christ; to be like Him, to be pure and transparent, to be holy, and to love with a pure love.

Many profess belief in the Bible but don't really believe that its words will have any bearing on their eternal destiny. The Bible has much to say about works. Certainly we aren't saved by works, but they shall determine our eternal reward. After all, it is written that faith without works is dead. Works are the way we prove the sincerity of our faith. But I've met so many people in my years of walking with the Lord who seem confident that no matter how they live their lives on the earth they will somehow make it to heaven and even receive their eternal reward.

*"Now if anyone build on this foundation with <u>gold, silver, and precious stones, wood, hay, and straw,</u> each one's work will become clear; for the Day will declare it, because it will be revealed by fire; and the fire will test each one's work, of what sort it is. If anyone's work he has built on it endures, he will receive a reward. If anyone's work is burned, he will suffer loss; but he himself will be saved, yet so as through fire"* **(1 Cor 3:12-15).**

What will make each of our individual works clear is the fire of God's holiness. It will take holy fire to reveal the motives behind our works. Our motives play a big part in determining if our works are gold, silver, and precious stones or wood, hay, and stubble. Some believer's works shall be burned, and he will suffer loss. Yes, the Bible says loss! *We don't often think that there will be any loss for the believer who makes it to heaven, but the Word of God tells us differently.* I don't know about you, but I don't want that to be my lot and portion.

Every believer needs to live with a daily consciousness of finishing his race and fulfilling God's plan for his life. I sort of have this picture in my mind of two graphs in heaven; one represents what I actually did with my life in God, and the other tells me what the fullness of God's plan and will was for me. And my constant pressing is to shorten the gap between the two.

At this point certain people may be thinking, "that's alright if I lose my reward because I'll still make it to heaven, and that's what's important." I'll be plain here and tell you that this is a loser's mentality. *A wise man considers the afterlife and his eternal reward, but a fool does not.* A wise man realizes that his life on earth is very temporal, but eternity is forever. The issue in not just one of salvation, but of your personal love for Jesus and your standing throughout eternity. Will you have a seat close to Jesus for all of eternity?

There's a reason why the mother of James and John requested that they sit on the right and left hand of Jesus (Mat 20:20-23). There's a reason why Jesus promised His disciples thrones where they would be judges (Mat 19:28). To those who overcome He grants a seat with Him on His throne (Rev 3:21). There's a reason why Jesus promised more authority to him who is faithful both here and the hereafter (Lk 16:10-12). Paul spoke of crowns being laid up for him (2 Tim 4:8). He spoke of attaining unto a certain resurrection (Phil 3:11) that included more than just the general resurrection of the righteous.

Heaven is for the saved. No one without the new nature can enter into the holy atmosphere of heaven. But rewards are for the sanctified and for those who refused to deviate from the pursuit of their first love.

On the other hand, hell is for the devil and his demons and for all those who chose to live independently of God.

Let's live like these things are true.

# CHAPTER 12

# *Holiness and the Lord's Return*

*"But take heed to yourselves, <u>lest your hearts be weighed down</u> with carousing, drunkenness, and cares of this life, and that day come upon you unexpectedly. For it will come as a snare on all those who dwell on the face of the whole earth. <u>Watch therefore, and prays always</u> that you may be counted worthy to escape all these things that will come to pass, and to stand before the Son of Man"* (Lk 21:34-36).

*The world's system is turning up the heat and creating an environment that is suffocating the spirit of watchfulness and prayer in many believers today.* The consequences of not watching over our hearts will be un-preparedness and an un-readiness that will cause us to miss the return of the Lord, lose out on our eternal reward, and be trapped here on the earth during the tribulation period.

Many people's schedules, clocks, and calendars are not set according to a heavenly order. Their priorities are wrong. Many Christians are busy, busy, busy…tired, tired, tired…no time or surrender in prayer, no spiritual nourishment, and no rest. It's a vicious cycle that is feeding and strengthening the flesh and its desires. This cycle must be reversed for people's spirits to gain the ascendancy over the flesh in order to move into the flow of God in these last days.

I want to deal with two issues in keeping ourselves watchful and ready for the Lord's return.

## BUSY-NESS

Typical scenario: There are parents, both husband and wife, both with regular jobs, and with school age children. They get their children ready for school in the morning before sending them off, and then stop by the local Dunkin' Donuts to grab a quick coffee and maybe a bite to eat. They come home from a full day's work late in the afternoon. The house is messy so Mom cleans and tidies up a little bit while getting some laundry done. Dad has to pick up the car he dropped off at the mechanic shop earlier in the day and then pick up the mail at the Post Office. On the way home he picks up dinner for the family since Mom is too tired to cook. The kids are isolated at home with each one doing their own thing in their own little world. One has his headphones on listening to music, one is playing his video games, while yet another is arguing with Mom about the clothes she wants to wear to a friend's house this evening that she can't seem to find.

Then comes the weekend and finally time to catch up on all the other extra chores; time to get a little extra sleep and relaxation; time to indulge a little in some innocent or even not so innocent pleasures.

Day in and day out, weekend in and weekend out, this is how most people live. This is life in America and in some other nations as well for the average family. Much worse and even more stressful for some who have single parent homes or are in abusive, strife-filled situations. And sadly, it is not much different for Christians than non-Christians except for maybe a church service on Sundays.

*Life for most people is a constant whirlwind, carving out a living, trying to climb out of debt, or stay out of debt, pay bills, save up for the children's college education or retirement, remodel the home, etc. etc. etc.* This is what many consider normal life. But is it normal? Is it wrong? Is it sinful? Is it according to God's standards? Can we be less busy and live less tired with less stress? Give more time to prayer and the things of God without neglecting our personal responsibilities? Or is this all a part and parcel of the present culture and world we live in that cannot be changed?

Before we address those questions, notice that in the verse of scripture above, the warning Jesus gave has to do with our hearts being weighed down. That's the issue. That's what we have to guard against. What I find is that this kind of busy, hectic lifestyle has a tendency to squash intimacy with God, sensitivity to people, and nullify God's real purpose for our lives. That is what makes it wrong and below God's standards. Does it weigh down your heart where you are less watchful and prayerful? That is the question you should be asking. *How can you order your life so that you stay filled, fresh, and on-fire about the things of the Lord? That's the real issue here.* The same order doesn't work for everyone. We are all living different lives with different schedules. The main point is that you need to get your life and house in order, and put it in a position that is conducive to receiving from the Lord and making your spiritual supply to others.

One of the mistakes people often make is to base all their decisions and order of schedule around money. Solomon, speaking for the common man, said that money answers all things. That, however, is only true when your priorities are in order. For example, I know of low income families who raised their children in the ways of the Lord, many times doing without, and they are reaping huge benefits from their children now. On the other hand, I know wealthy families who used their money to live in more luxury, but their children are away from the Lord. Their money, which was used for their pleasures, led them away from the Lord's ways. How are you using your money, and what are your priorities?

Recently I had lunch with a wonderful brother who is a painter. It is a blue-collar job that does not pay real high wages. His wife is a homemaker who home schools their children. If they put their children in public school and the wife got an outside job, they would do much better financially. But their priorities are in order and they realize that money isn't everything. I admire a decision like that, and I know it pleases the Lord. The public school system is a gateway to hell for many of today's children. I know some who have made it through, but I know more that have not. You can't base all your decisions on money. Too many Christians are materialistic minded and earthly minded instead of eternity minded.

*"And the world will be as it was in the days of Lot. People went about their daily business—eating and drinking, buying and selling, farming and building—until the morning Lot left Sodom. Then fire and burning sulfur rained down from heaven and destroyed them all. Yes, it will be 'business as usual' right up to the day when the Son of Man is revealed"* (Luke 17:28-30—NLT).

This verse doesn't even talk about sin, which I will also mention later. None of these things listed—eating, drinking, buying, selling, farming (building), and planting—that people were doing in Lot's day were wrong in themselves, but the people were so absorbed in them that they had no time for spiritual matters.

There is great financial pressure today. The temptation to make quick money, even sometimes through questionable means, is very strong. You need to be assured that if God is first in your life He will take care of you (Mat 6:33). *If you learn to follow the Spirit of God He can teach you how to profit in all things, and that includes financial affairs. But if you choose to follow the system of the world and try and keep up financially with all the world's demands, you will miss God.*

The supreme call of the hour is to prepare yourself for the glory of the Lord and the harvest to come, and to be watchful and ready for the Lord's return. Get your house and priorities in order. Get filled with the Spirit of God and the Word of God. Win souls, win souls, and win more souls! People are eternal and far more important than possessions. Put yourself in a position to be the witness God has called you to be. Remember that busyness is not always a sign of effectiveness.

## SIN

This is another issue that stops Christians from being watchful and having a spirit of prayer and readiness for the Lord. I want to continue being very practical and honest with you as I share my heart. At this writing, I've been saved for over 30 years and preached my first message back in 1983. I've watched my generation be raised and I've watched my generation raise their children. *There is great failure today in this area of raising our children in true holiness and the fear of the Lord. This is why many of our children are being lost to the world.*

Chewing gum was a big no-no in school 50 years ago. Today it's drugs, rampant sexual promiscuity, and even murder. The standard has fallen. The Church has followed the world and lowered her own standards. As a result, the home has lowered her standards. The course of generations is always affected by sin and the choices of the previous generation. If not for the mercy of God, many of us would be casualties too. But when one knows better, when one has been enlightened, there is great responsibility to walk in that light and a great accountability to the Lord.

I have been a guest in other ministers' homes and got up to use the bathroom in the nighttime and observed the minister's teenagers watching pornography on the television, or nowadays on computer. I've heard the music that minister's kids listen to today and I am appalled. I've been in the homes of local church deacons and elders and have observed very suggestive magazines, novels, and videos that I would never have in my home. I have seen a level of rebellion and disrespect in today's children that was almost unknown in my generation. What is going on? *Strong godly leadership in the Church and in the home is at an all time low.*

As a leader in the church or in our home, we not only have a great responsibility as gatekeepers to watch what comes into our own lives and homes, but also over those the Lord has entrusted to us. One day we will give account to the Lord for the souls entrusted to our care (Heb 13:17). *We must be thorough in holding up the standard so people can keep out the spirit of the world and sin from their lives.* I've seen leaders make very unwise choices in this area simply because they underestimate the power and gravity of sin and its effects.

Since the young generation is the future of the Church and the nation, let me give you an example in this area of how a little leaven can leaven the whole lump. That is, a little sin, a little poison, a little cancer, can destroy the whole body or the entire life. It can set a person's life completely off course.

One day when our son was 12 years of age he came home from youth group and told me how his youth pastor had found one of the other kid's iPods and discovered worldly music on it. One mother said that it's not so bad, and it won't hurt for them to listen to a little secular music. A parent who says that has no understanding of how the devil works.

My wife had a word from the Lord she received in a dream. The dream was a prophetic warning for a large church we were preaching in. In the dream she saw music coming out of a CD that was bringing devils into the church. Music has power to transmit that kind of influence.

This sort of thing is happening everywhere in churches especially among the young people. But again, the responsibility lies with parents and the spiritual leadership in churches. What kind of example are we setting? And what kind of training are we giving them? Are we entertaining them, or are we really preparing them spiritually to be a soldier for Christ in this life?

I'm amazed at how we downplay the spirit of the world in our churches today. I've seen pastors get up and promote rated R movies and not think anything of it. I've seen women who have been part of the church for years dress so scantily. I've seen supposed Christian youth concerts where teens are bumping and grinding to the music (for those of you who don't know what bumping and grinding is, it is the equivalent of having sexual intercourse with your clothes on). And what do most Christian leaders do about things like this? Absolutely nothing. Why?

Because they are afraid to offend people. They would rather offend God and please the devil. I know I'm being strong here, but it's time to speak plain about these things. We are losing a generation.

We are living in the end times. *Holiness and the fear of the Lord are to be major emphases as we approach the rapture and the Lord's return.* Let me conclude by listing several scriptures that bear this out. Pay close attention to the theme of holiness as it relates to the end times.

*Husbands, love your wives, just as Christ also loved the church and gave Himself for her, that He might sanctify and cleanse her with the washing of water by the word, that He might present her to Himself a glorious church, not having spot or wrinkle or any such thing, but that she should be holy and without blemish.* (Eph 5:25-27)

*And may the Lord make you increase and abound in love to one another and to all, just as we do to you, so that He may establish your hearts blameless in holiness before our God and Father at the coming of our Lord Jesus Christ with all His saints.* (1 Thes 3:12-13)

*Now may the God of peace Himself sanctify you completely; and may your whole spirit, soul, and body be preserved blameless at the coming of our Lord Jesus Christ.* (1 Thes 5:23)

*I urge you in sight of God who gives life to all things, and before Christ Jesus who witnessed the good confession before Pontius Pilate, that you keep this commandment without spot, blameless until our Lord Jesus Christ's appearing...* (1 Tim 6:13-14)

*For the grace of God that brings salvation has appeared to all men, teaching us that, denying ungodliness and worldly lusts, we should live soberly, righteously, and godly in the present age, looking for the blessed hope and glorious appearing of our great God and Savior Jesus Christ...* (Tit 2:11-13)

*And let us consider one another in order to stir up love and good works, not forsaking the assembling of ourselves together, as is the manner of some, but exhorting one another, and so much the more as you see the Day approaching.* (Heb 10:24-25)

*Therefore, since all these things will be dissolved, what manner of persons ought you to be in holy conduct and godliness, looking for and hastening the coming of the day of God, because of which the heavens will be dissolved, being on fire, and the elements will melt with fervent heat? Nevertheless we, according to His promise, look for new heavens and a new earth in which righteousness dwell. Therefore, beloved, looking forward to these things, be diligent to be found by Him in peace, without spot and blameless...* (2 Pet 3:11-14)

*But the anointing which you have received from Him abides in you, and you do not need that anyone teach you; but as the same anointing teaches you concerning all things, and is true, and is not a lie, and just as it has taught you, you will abide in Him. And now, little children, abide in Him, that when He appears, we may have confidence and not be ashamed before Him at His coming.* (1 John 2:27-28)

*Beloved, now we are children of God; and it has not yet been revealed what we shall be, but we know that when He is revealed, we shall be like Him, for we shall see Him as He is. And everyone who has this hope in Him purifies himself, just as He is pure.* (1 John 3:2-3)

*Love has been perfected among us in this: that we may have boldness in the Day of Judgment; because as He is, so are we in this world.* (1 John 4:17)

As you can plainly see, holiness needs to be a major issue in the Church especially as time draws nearer to the return of the Lord. This is a matter of eternal life and eternal death. Watch and pray. Be a wise gatekeeper. In doing so you will save both yourself and many others by helping them turn from the error of their ways to righteousness.

## CHAPTER 13

# *The Holy Spirit and Personal Holiness*

When the great apostle of faith Smith Wigglesworth was once asked about the secret of his close walk with God he replied: "The Holy Spirit and personal holiness." What a word! His answer speaks volumes. These are the two streams of our life in God. These two components of our faith are what will make us stalwart Christians!

Think of it: The Holy Spirit has been sent to help us in every area of life. Jesus told us that He, the Holy Spirit, would speak to us whatsoever He hears, lead us and guide us into all truth, and show us things to come (John 16:13). What a promise! Is it a reality to you? Jesus also told us that the Holy Spirit would not speak of Himself but would testify of Jesus and glorify Him. What an inheritance we have in this promise of the Father that Jesus foretold for us! Greater is He who is in us than He who is in the world (1 John 4::4). Be filled with the Spirit!

Being full of the Spirit is the perfect order of God for our lives. Time in the Word and time in the spirit of prayer, praise, and prophecy is what will fill you up. It is sad to say that most Christians today neglect this area of fellowship. This is the reason for the weak and anemic state of much of the Church in this hour.

When your aim is to be full of the Spirit of God you are right on course with God's plan for your life. This is the highest position a Christian can take in his walk with God. To be full of the Spirit means that you are full of God—full of revelation, power, utterance, life, love, peace, joy, patience, goodness and all that the Holy Spirit is.

To be full of the Spirit is also the way to walk in holiness because it is through the Spirit that you mortify the deeds of your body (Rom 8:13), and keep the flesh under. That is how you set yourself apart from the world and that is what holiness is. It is the character and likeness of God. It's when you are full of God that you are most like Him and most set apart and distinct from the world.

I have found that when the Church departs from the fullness of the Spirit filled life (Eph 5:18-19) and does not pursue holiness (Heb 12:14), the devil gets in. The flesh and the world begin their domination. Life in the Spirit is not rocket science. Feed your flesh, walk in the lusts of the flesh, and you will be ruled by the flesh and never fulfill God's plan for your life. On the other hand, if you will feed your spirit, walk in the Spirit, and live in the Spirit, you will fulfill God's plan for your life.

Christians have problems overcoming their flesh because of neglect to give themselves over to fellowship with God. Some are trying to fight their sins and habits in the flesh through strong resolve and the efforts of their own will. It won't last. The way to overcome the lust of the flesh, the lust of the eyes, and the pride of life is to get filled up with God.

What would make Christians not want to fellowship with God? I believe the greatest hindrance to fellowship with God is a wrong image of God or a lack of revelation concerning God's love for you. When you receive a revelation of how much God loves you and how much He longs to fellowship with you, you will melt like ice in the fire and you will not be able to resist the Lord.

Here is a great verse depicting God's desire to fellowship with you:

*"I, even I, am He who blots out your transgressions FOR MY OWN SAKE..."* (Isa 43:25).

The above verse tells us that the Lord blotted out Israel's sins, not for their sake, but for His own sake. I thought sins blotted out benefitted the sinner and not God. What does this mean? Among other things, this verse speaks of how God acted on His desire to fellowship with man. You see, as long as man remains in his sin God cannot fellowship with him for Isaiah 59:2 states that man's sin separates him from God. God's desire to fellowship with man has always been so great that He removed sin, the biggest obstacle to our fellowship with God. Hallelujah!

What is it in the heart of God that desires fellowship with man? He wants to be with you 24/7, and that is exactly why He sent the Holy Spirit into your heart. His passion for your presence is stronger than your passion for His. Let that last statement sink into your spirit.

Here is another verse that shows us the desire of the Lord to fellowship with us:

*"And when the hour had come, Jesus reclined at table, and the apostles with him. And he said to them, <u>I have earnestly and intensely desired</u> to eat this Passover with you before I suffer; for I say unto you, I shall eat it no more until it is fulfilled in the kingdom of God"* (Lk 22:14-16 Amp).

The Passover was originally a feast for those about to be delivered from the oppression of their enemies. Israel celebrated the Passover at the beginning of each Jewish New Year to mark the beginning of Israel's new life as a people. It served as the final dynamic proof of God's presence and protection. The Passover is characterized by selecting a lamb, which is sacrificed four days later and eaten as part of a major commemorative meal. Passover was also a judgment against all the gods of Egypt.

Now here is Jesus, the Lamb of God, four days before He would offer up His own body as a sacrifice for sin, and as judgment against Satan. On that fourth day the veil of the temple would be torn in two signifying that the presence of God would no longer be confined to a temple made with human hands, but could now inhabit the temple (body) of man. Wow! This is why the desire of the Lord was so earnest and intense. He knew what was coming! And He knew that although the disciples could no longer fellowship with Him in the flesh, they could through His own blood sacrifice have unbroken fellowship with Him, by the Holy Spirit, who would soon indwell them and rest upon them. Hallelujah! And thus the desire of God for every man would be fulfilled!

If you are living in sin you are under condemnation. Your fellowship with God is blocked. But as soon as you repent and forsake your sin, and turn toward Jesus Christ you can have a feast just as the prodigal son did (Lk 15:11-32).

When the prodigal son confessed his sin and returned to his father's house, the father went out to meet him even when the son was a great distance away. This tells you that the father was probably out there every day looking for the hour when his son would return home. I'm sure the father thought of his wayward son each and every hour of each and every day. How he longed for his son's return and for his son's fellowship! This is one of the most beautiful pictures of the yearning and intense desire that is in God the Father's heart for fellowship with His children.

The prodigal son's father was not satisfied with just the older son's fellowship. Each one of God's children is unique to God and He longs for fellowship with each of us. Can you sense His heart's yearning to fellowship with you? Can you sense His overwhelming love for you? Can you also see why the devil works full time at distorting the image of God through the use of religion, legalism, dead traditions, and lies about God? If you don't know God's heart the devil will take advantage of you by heaping on you guilt, condemnation, and shame. He will also use the world and all that is in the world to distract us from the heart of God. Like a wily fox, the devil is constantly seeking to break up that union and that fellowship that each of us should be enjoying with God. He knows that without that vital link of communion with God you will never fulfill God's perfect will for your life.

Let me say this: If you are not enjoying the Lord, something is wrong. Perhaps the fault lies here in your image of God and lack of revelation of God's love and desire to fellowship with you.

Broken fellowship with the Lord is one of the greatest reasons for man's failures. Every wrong in our lives is a direct by-product of neglected fellowship with the Lord.

Once you understand God's love for you it is a natural response to want to return that same love back to Him. All God wants from you is your love…your heart. Isn't this what all mere human beings also seek from each other?

Responding to the Lord's love and desire for you is how you begin to live the Spirit-filled life and a walk of holiness. When you love someone you want to know him. You want to please him. You want to be with him.

When the Bridegroom returns it will be the unreserved response of the Bride's burning love for Him that will catch her away in a moment of time to be with Him forever. All others will be left behind to suffer through the great tribulation (see the parable of the 10 virgins in Matthew 25:1-13). Shouldn't your heart be responding to the Lord's love a little bit more?

CHAPTER 14

# *Preparing for the Lord's Return*

Everyone who has eternal life is going on with Jesus in the rapture, whether it be in the first-fruits rapture (pre-tribulation view—Mat 25: 1-13) or in the final harvest at the end of the tribulation (post-tribulation view—Mat 24:29-31; Rev 14:14-16). If you are a student of the Word, you can see that there is a split church at the rapture where one is taken and another is left, and you can also readily see that Mat 24:29-31 and Mat 25:1-13 are two different events. In Revelation 13 and 14 we see many saints in heaven while other saints on the earth are being martyred for the faith before Jesus comes for the final harvest. If you have eternal life in you, you will go either way, in either event.

Do you honestly think that the five foolish virgins were doomed for eternal destruction because they missed the first-fruits rapture? They were virgins, born again, righteous, pure, and had lamps (the light of the Word), but were simply not prepared when the Bridegroom delayed His coming. They were, however, still God's children, not hypocrites or workers of lawlessness whom Jesus *never* knew like those found in Mat 7:21-23. All Jesus told the foolish virgins was that He did not know them. In other words, He did not know them intimately.

The entire lesson of the parable is to be ready for the Bridegroom's coming. How do you stay ready? By buying extra oil. What do you buy oil with? Money. Money represents your life. Oil represents the Holy Spirit. No, you cannot purchase the Holy Spirit with money, but you must submit your life to Him. The five wise virgins purchased extra oil in addition to what they already had in their lamps. They used extra money to purchase extra oil. The foolish virgins kept the reserve funds for themselves instead of purchasing extra oil. In other words, they held back a part of their lives while the wise virgins surrendered all. *The lesson is clear: the way you stay ready is by staying full of the Spirit (oil). And you can't stay full unless you've surrendered your life to Jesus.* Without personal revival you cannot be full and stay full, and you'll miss the first-fruits rapture.

There is a call for repentance going out right now for all those who have not surrendered their lives to Jesus. The one great mark and characteristic of the Bride will be her unreserved response to the love of the Bridegroom. There are many Christians who serve Jesus wholeheartedly, but there are also many who praise Him with their lips while their hearts are far from Him (Mat 15:8). There are many who profess Christ but in works they deny Him (Titus 1:16).

With all the gospel and all the Word that goes out on the airwaves of America, much of the general populace still does not know what a real Christian even is. Why is this? Because there's been too much of the world in the Church, and her impact has been limited. *We must understand that our greatest impact on the world will come when we are least like the world.* The Church's power is in her distinction. What will turn lives around in the Church is when Christians become disciples. The proof of true conversion is that we are following the Lord, and that the world knows us by our love (John 13:35).

One of the greatest challenges of being a Christian today is to serve the Lord without distractions. This is a key in staying full of the Spirit, and staying ready for Jesus' soon return. This is what Paul told the Corinthians.

*"But this I say, brethren, the time is short, so that from now on even those who have wives should be as though they had none, those who weep as though they did not weep, those who rejoice as though they did not rejoice, those who buy as though they did not possess, and those who use this world as not misusing it. For the form of this world is passing away"* **(1 Cor 7:29-31).**

These verses simply mean that because of the nature and spirit of this age and of the reality of the coming of Jesus, believers are to adopt the attitude of finding their source in Christ and serving Him without distractions. Instead of putting your hope of eternity in earthly institutions, whether marriage, the social sphere, or the economic world, you put all your hope and trust in the Lord. This speaks of our consecration to Him.

When a believer is wholly consecrated to the Lord, he finds life only in His words, and he becomes filled with what Jesus says. He truly becomes your Bread of life. It becomes rapturous to be filled with His words. You live in a state of rapture with your heart yearning for more of His life, more of His words, and more of His Spirit.

Eternal life is to know Him (John 17:3). When Jesus returns He will come for that *life. It's not your body or your natural man that Jesus is coming for, but it is for the life in you.* Your burning heart, your inward hunger, and longing cry are what Jesus is returning for. If you are found pursuing the spirit of the world when He comes, or you have been totally distracted by the cares of this life, then you are not going with Him. Jesus is drawn to that *eternal life* that is in you. That is Him in you. It is not so much you He is coming for, but rather what has been created in you.

You may legally and positionally have that life, but have you entered into it? Is His life eating up the mortality in you? What is mortality? It is not the physical body, but it is all that hinders and all that is contrary to the life and nature of God in you. The New Testament has 66 different descriptions of mortality: such as seditions, heresy, strife, envy, malice, hatred, murder, emulation, witchcraft, covetousness, adultery, fornications, etc. etc. etc. The following verse bears this out:

*"For we who are in this tent groan, being burdened, not because we want to be unclothed, but further clothed, that mortality may be swallowed up by life"* **(1 Cor 5:4).**

This is the rapture position. It is a marvelous truth. We, who are in this earthly body, groan for deliverance from it, not that we should die, but that we should have more of God's Spirit. Is this your heart's longing? Are you hungry for communion with the Lord? Are you caught up in Him? If so, then mortality is being eaten up in you, and you are entering into more of His life. It is God's wonderful plan that the whole of our lives should be filled with God. This is true Pentecost as we see it in Acts 2 where believers were in the temple daily praising and blessing God (Lk 24:52-53). *Oh! Oh! Oh! This is it! To live in rapture before you're actually raptured!*

I have read Smith Wigglesworth's books for many years. I'm just catching up with some of that beloved man's revelations. The revelation Wigglesworth had on the rapture is so profound. Here it is: *"All those who will be caught up are going to be eaten up, their old natures, old desires, and old lives are going to be eaten up with His life, so that when Jesus comes His life will meet the life that is in them."*

Isn't that powerful? God wants us ready for translation! The process we are in now is to build up our lives on the lines of readiness. This doesn't mean absolute perfection where we never sin again or fall short of God's perfect will, but it means that we are pressing on to be further clothed with God's Spirit where you are seeking a deeper experience in God, a deeper separation from the world, a holier and more perfect place where you and Christ are one.

As a former sinner, have you ever been drunk on wine, beer, or hard liquor? The state of rapture is that you are drunk on the Spirit of God, drunk on His holiness, drunk with His likeness…having a fulness of joy and an unshakeable peace that surpasses all understanding. Here is another quote from Wigglesworth on being drunk with the Spirit that blessed me immeasurably: "*We can be so filled with the Spirit, so clothed upon by Him, so purified within, so made ready for the rapture, that all the time we are drunk.*"

Now this didn't mean that Wigglesworth acted weird and crazy all the time. He said that he could be sober one minute when he needed to be with others or when his drunkenness drew criticism, and enter right back into being drunk the next minute according to the occasion. What a life!!! You can't live this kind of life in sin or in pursuit of the world. *You can't enjoy this kind of liberty in the Holy Ghost on a consistent basis unless you walk in holiness, for holiness is the habitation of God and His Spirit.* This is the height of the Spirit-filled life God wants us to enjoy. By God's amazing empowerment of grace believers can access and live this Spirit-filled life.

I don't know about you, but this is what I'm going after. May it be that this attitude abounds in multitudes of believers across the nations where their new nature groans and travails to be delivered from the body and further clothed with the Spirit until the saints in large numbers will be crying out, *"Come, Lord Jesus!"*

That is when the trumpet will sound, and we'll all go home! What a day that will be! That, my friends is the rapture.

Are you ready???

# CHAPTER 15

# The Judgment Seat of Christ

*"And, behold, I come quickly; and my reward is with me, to give to every man according as his work shall be"* **(Revelation 22:12).**

Several years ago the Lord began dealing with me about preaching on "lost themes" (the end times, the rapture, the second coming of Christ, heaven, hell, holiness, the judgments of God, etc.). He said that there's got to be more preaching on these themes for they are emphasized in the Scriptures. He said that there has been a diabolical silence on these topics. As I studied the Word of God I was amazed at how much content and emphasis is given to these vital themes. When is the last time you heard preaching on these themes?

One of the great themes I've given much thought to recently is concerning the judgment seat of Christ. This judgment does not involve our salvation but our works and subsequent rewards. Each act of our lives has been recorded and will be judged from the standpoint of both our zeal and our motives. All our works will be weighed on the basis of whether we have labored for the love and glory of God or for self-praise and the glory of man (Mat 6:1-6, 16-18). What have we built on the foundation of Jesus Christ? Have we given the Lord gold, silver and precious stones, or wood, hay and stubble (1 Cor 3:12)? Are our lives filled with hidden motives of pride, or pure motives of love?

The Word of God has much to say about crowns and rewards. For instance, did you know that there are at least five types of crowns mentioned in the scriptures? Here they are:

1. Incorruptible crown (1 Cor 9:25): A crown given to those who have kept their bodies under subjection.

2. Crown of rejoicing (1 Thes 2:19-20): A crown given to the soul winner.

3. Crown of glory (1 Pet 5:4): A crown given for full time service.

4. Crown of life (Rev 2:10): A crown given to the martyr.

5. Crown of righteousness (2 Tim 4:8): A crown given to those who love His appearing.

Did you know that at the judgment seat of Christ there will be terror (2 Cor 5:9-11), loss (1 Cor 3:15) and shame (1 John 2:28) for some believers? That is a solemn thought.

Did you know that in the world to come men will achieve different positions (Lk 19:11-19, Mat 25:23)? There will be a great difference in the rank and honor received by the saints in the next age. Man will not be rewarded or promoted on the basis of his natural talents and capabilities, but rather on his faithfulness to what was given him. Works that are done in faith, in love, and by the leading of the Holy Spirit will stand the test of God's fire.

Above all these things, the apostle Paul hints of yet a greater prize which he himself was seeking.

*"If by any means I might attain unto the resurrection of the dead...I press toward the mark for the prize of the high calling of God in Christ Jesus"* (Phil 3:11, 14).

What is this prize that Paul exerted all his efforts to attain? It appears that he was seeking diligently to be a part of a first-fruits resurrection. The Scriptures teach that there is a definite order to the resurrection (1 Cor 15:22-23). Many believers don't even realize that this is a prize to be won. If the apostle Paul was making every effort to attain to this prize, how much more ought we?

What is necessary to attain unto this first-fruits resurrection? Note Phil 3:7-10. In spite of all that Paul had attained to in ministry—visions and revelations, miracles, churches planted, ministry workers raised up—at the end of his life he was still in hot pursuit of yet a greater prize—to win Christ, to gain Christ, to know Him! This is more than salvation. Did you know that this is the greatest prize—to win closeness to Christ throughout eternity? Not every believer will have achieved an eternal position close to Christ. Just as it was during Jesus' earth walk, so will it be throughout eternity that each follower will fall into a special group and classification. Jesus had 500 disciples, and then 70 closer, and then 12 even closer, and then the 3 who were closest to Him, and finally John the beloved who was Jesus' closest disciple and friend. Let me tell you that my heart burns every time I ponder these things.

*"...You are God's building...I have laid the foundation, and another builds on it. But let each one take heed how he builds on it. If anyone's work which he has built on it endures, he will receive a reward"* **(1 Cor 3:9, 10, 14).**

Did you also know that God uses things we give Him here on earth to add to the substance of heaven? God put David's tears in a heavenly bottle and wrote them in a heavenly book (Ps 56:8). God took Cornelius' prayers and money and translated them into a memorial in heaven (Acts 10:4). The prayers of the saints are transformed into heavenly incense before the throne (Rev 5:8). The righteous acts of the saints are translated into fine linen to array the Lamb's wife (Rev 19:8). Know that every sacrifice and trial you handle in Christ here on the earth is translated into building material for God in heaven. All our earthly victories and maturity in Christ will add heavenly materiality to our spiritual house in heaven (1 Pet 2:5).

Our new home in heaven (John 14:2) will be established according to the works we build on the foundation of Jesus Christ while on the earth. Even the heavenly city of Jerusalem is being built with our earthly works of gold, silver, and precious stones with the wall of the city having its foundations serving as a memorial to the lives of the apostles (Rev 21:14). Isn't it interesting that the New Jerusalem is called the Bride of Christ (Rev 21: 2, 9-11)? That's because the entire city is made with materials furnished by real men and women of God who lived consecrated and surrendered lives to God.

Dear friends, there are times we may wonder if the Lord really sees every trial we endure and sacrifice we make to serve Him, but be assured that He does. And if we want to be wise servants, we would do well to consider our reward and eternal position.

"*Do you not know that those who run in a race all run, but* one receives the prize? *Run in such a way that you may obtain it*" (1 Cor 9:24).

Let us run to win.

CHAPTER 16

# *Spiritual Dangers*

I see a number of dangers in the Western Church today. These dangers pertain to the latter times and I address them for the purpose of admonition and correction, not criticism.

*"Now the Spirit speaks expressly that <u>in the latter times</u> some will depart from the faith..." (1 Tim 4:1).*

A departure from the faith in the latter times means that the lifestyles of professing Christians will not support their confession. Notice these next three verses:

*"For [although] they hold a form of piety (true religion), they deny and reject and are strangers to the power of it <u>[their conduct belies the genuineness of their profession]</u>" (2 Tim 3:5).*

*"They profess to know God, but <u>in works they deny Him</u>..." (Titus 1:16).*

*"These people draw near to Me with their mouth, and honor Me with their lips, <u>but their heart is far from Me</u>"* (Mat 15:8).

Here is God's solution for a departure from the faith:

*"<u>Preach the word!</u> Be ready in season and out of season. Convince, rebuke, exhort, with all long-suffering and teaching. For the time will come when they will not endure <u>sound doctrine</u>..."* (2 Tim 4:3).

*"And they continued steadfastly <u>in the apostles' doctrine and fellowship</u>, in the breaking of bread, and in prayers"* (Acts 2:42).

Character in conduct and conversation will be forever attached to sound doctrine. Today we are seeing a widespread departure from sound doctrine and the faith of our forefathers. Holiness and sanctification are at an all time low in the Western church. This is because in the Western mind-set knowledge and application of the Scriptures are disconnected. In the Bible and in the culture of the kingdom of God, however, they are one and the same.

Biblical holiness and true discipleship are lacking in the lives of many professing Christians. Many preachers no longer equate holiness with sound doctrine. It is becoming more and more uncommon to minister correction and reproof to people for fear of offending them. How many Christians do you honestly know whose aim is to live without spot and blemish and who purpose and pursue daily to be a part of the glorious Bride of Christ?

# THE DUAL LIFE OF MINISTERS

The first place I see danger is in the ministers themselves. The example of leadership is so important. It is popular today to forego or soften the character qualifications required for those aspiring to church leadership (1 Tim 3). Instead, the talents/gifts, education, and the charisma of individuals are subtly given preeminence and esteemed above character.

The Scriptures, however, do not separate sound doctrine from behavior and conduct. In Paul's epistles, especially to younger ministers Timothy and Titus, he emphasizes character and always equates it with sound doctrine. In other words, you cannot have one without the other, and church leaders are held to a higher standard of it. Paul's defense of the gospel usually included something about his personal life and character and the things he had suffered to preach the gospel. In the Western Church there is very little emphasis on this. So what happens when the sins of ministers are exposed, and the public finds out that for years their leaders have been living a dual life? We've seen too many of examples of this in the last 30 years. The result is that people, in general, begin to lose faith in the ministry, and the Word of God becomes void in their lives.

Failure to understand the true servant role of ministers has led to the exaltation of their positions to unhealthy "superstar" and "celebrity" status. I'm afraid much of television ministry has hurt the cause of the Church in this regard. This is the image of Christianity, at least here in the West, and it is peddled throughout the nations. This image has hurt our cause.

Ministers are to serve the Church in a sacrificial way, resisting the worship of their followers, and the temptation to control their lives and lord it over them. Many are insecure and would never admit that they have a problem in this area. The Spirit of the Lord spoke to me one time and said, *"The grip of the spirit of control is the desire for an honored reputation."* The desire for an honored reputation disqualifies you from having a higher grade of fellowship with Jesus who made Himself of no reputation (Phil 2:7).

A number of years ago at a charismatic conference in an East Coast city, a pastor stood on a stage in front of a large crowd and smugly announced that the guest speaker was more than an apostle. Then the host asked everyone to bow down to the person, claiming that this posture was necessary to release God's power. "This is the only way you can receive this kind of anointing!" the host declared, bowing in front of the speaker. Immediately, about 80 percent of the audience fell prostrate on the floor. Only a smaller percentage walked out or stood in silent protest. Can you believe it?

This, no doubt, is an extreme example of idolatry, but this attitude is prevalent in the West. We've lost sight of the teachings and practices of Jesus (John 13:3-15). Christian ministers should never exude pride and arrogance. Humility should be our mantle, and it must begin with leaders everywhere.

Have you ever asked yourself this question: *"Why do most people desire to minister in their gifts above their personal relationship with God?"* Why do people esteem talent above character? Isn't it because they desire an honored reputation above relationship? Isn't the root of this a desire to be seen by men and honored by men rather than a private life with God as Jesus first taught (Mat 6)? Pure religion is caring for orphans and widows while remaining unspotted from the world (Jam 1:27). Why aren't many believers fulfilled in doing this? Isn't a large part of it because of the wrong example and image many of us have had of ministry?

The private life of many ministers either qualifies or disqualifies them to be a leader in the Church. What has happened in this country with many of the bigger and more influential ministries is that they've gotten into the luxury and prosperity of American Christianity while becoming lax in their private prayer lives and consecration. Even though pulpit ministers are in the limelight they need to continually crucify the desire for an honored reputation among men while resurrecting and feeding the desire for private priestly ministry. Without a Christ-like example of leadership, there will continue to be a dilution of character in the Church.

Am I saying that most ministers are ungodly and sinful? No, not at all. There's a minority, I think, that have very serious problems and addictions, but most of them probably have a genuine love for God. On the other hand, I also believe there are thousands of false ministers who are wolves in sheep's clothing. What is for certain is that many are lacking the character qualities necessary to lead the Church. After years in the traveling ministry and going to thousands of churches the late Kenneth Hagin stated that he had known very few who actually qualified to be pastors of those churches. Many were anointed, but did not possess the character qualities necessary to function in their respective ministries (1 Tim 3). Think about that.

# THE PREACHING OF THE REAL GOSPEL WITH POWER

The second danger I see in the Church today, most notably in the Western Church, is the area of substituting media driven ministry, entertainment, and social services for the real preaching of the gospel. Our methods have diluted our message. Undoubtedly, methods change according to the character of each generation, but our message should not.

In an effort to reach the younger generation there is a trend I've witnessed over the last two decades that skews strongly toward entertainment and a watered down version of the gospel. Mid-week youth meetings in many churches now consist of video and arcade games with an actual service that resembles a rock concert followed by a nice 10-minute speech/pep talk about spirituality, then a return to the games. Some people on staff at a large church said recently that their large youth services have the feel of herding livestock instead of developing disciples through close-knit relationships with the kids. At this writing the largest seeker-friendly church in the nation now boasts of 9500 affiliate churches. The basic culture of the seeker friendly churches says that it's alright to be a believer in Jesus without being a true disciple and adhering to the Lord's ways. There is no confrontation of sin and worldliness, and a challenge to go deeper in the Christian walk.

Personally, it is a great disappointment to witness the love of the world in so many believers, the dullness toward spiritual things, the lack of interest in truly adhering to the life of Christ and teachings of the Scriptures. I long for relationships with people who desire a greater consecration in being true disciples of the Lord, and have a heart hunger for the glory of His presence. I long for greater transparency and accountability in my own friendships for transparency is the very essence of holiness.

Over the years I've witnessed far too many outreaches and church events where social services are provided for people (which Jesus commanded us to do, and which we should always provide…feed the hungry, clothe the naked, visit the sick and imprisoned, etc.), but the gospel is hardly ever preached, and when it is, it is usually a nice pep talk emphasizing only the benefits of Christianity without any mention of the other aspects of the gospel. The Law, which the old-timers skillfully used to bring a sinner to Christ, is sadly missing from our gospel presentation. Christians have been falsely taught to believe that the good news of the gospel is all that is necessary. But how can the good news of Jesus Christ be appreciated without the knowledge of the law revealing people's sin (Rom 3:20)? After all, the law is the tutor to bring sinners to Christ (Gal 3:24). How can a person appreciate the cure for sin if he doesn't believe he's sick?

When Paul had audience with the governor Felix he reasoned with him concerning righteousness, self-control, and the judgment to come (Acts 24:25). Felix trembled and asked Paul to leave. Was any part of Paul's message to this sinner what we are hearing today in our gospel? *I understand that the character of the age has changed, and people are easily offended by plain preaching, but this should present both a challenge and an opportunity to acquire wisdom to preach the timeless truths of the gospel in a gracious way and still without compromise.*

I'm afraid we've been catering to the liberal sector of America in not preaching the full and balanced gospel. Political correctness and an ungodly tolerance have crept into our gospel and have given birth to the fear and intimidation of man. We must understand that the liberal spirit has no set of absolutes, so they can justify doing whatever they want. A society that has no absolutes also has no discernment and every man begins to do what is right in their own eyes. A lack of absolutes in one generation leads to the moral decay of future generations and an inability to discern between good and evil. This is why we need to put an emphasis on character and holiness in the Church. This is why we need to confront sin and worldliness. This is why we need to exalt the person of Jesus Christ, and live as He lived. This is why we need to preach the gospel with signs and wonders, and allow the Holy Spirit to move in our meetings and in our lives.

God is waiting for the obedience of His people. There is a harvest waiting to be reaped. Many are ready to receive salvation through the love and power of God.

## RELATIONSHIP-BASED CHRISTIANITY

The third and final area I'd like to address is the danger of not maintaining a depth in our relationships with other believers who desire to grow and with those outside of Christ. From the beginning God has always moved in relationships. *Too much structure in the Church without sufficient relationship can kill life.* We have to train ourselves to follow the life-giving flow of the Spirit and then add structure where necessary. Spirit should always have preeminence over structure.

Jesus walked with His disciples. Jesus dined with sinners. Christianity did not begin with huge edifices and organizations created by the dictates of men. It began with relationships. It began with just being together. I believe the reason so many of our big influential leaders appear to be untouchable and unapproachable is because of the element of fathering and discipleship that is missing from the ministry. That is also the reason for a lack of true accountability.

Individual empowerment and relationship-based Christianity are what many believers are hungering for today. Young people are especially tired of religious politics, hypocrisy, irrelevant preaching, and a lack of personal discipleship. Many of our churches today are losing touch with the cries of the younger generation. There are fundamental flaws in the pyramid structure of the traditional Church that keeps personal discipleship and individual empowerment at a low level. We've got to be more open and flexible to a paradigm shift in the Church that will give place to more of these things. In the New Testament I see a Church government that promotes both responsibility and liberty in the individual priesthood of every believer. I see less emphasis on structure, programs, and personalities, but more emphasis on relationship, community, and the ministry gifts and anointing of the Holy Spirit.

Relational dynamics must be restored to every stream of ministry. Spiritual and not carnal fellowship must have priority. Carnal fellowship is centered on a party spirit and social time only, with entertainment as the focus, but spiritual fellowship revolves around loving and encouraging one another in daily life and the things of the Lord. Carnal fellowship leaves you empty, but spiritual fellowship leaves you edified.

We must not allow programs to replace people, and technology to take the place of personal encounters. The great commission will not be fulfilled without the element of relationship-based evangelism and discipleship. The Church is primarily organic and grows from within. Relational dynamics are necessary to accomplish this.

The purpose of God's power is to change lives by learning and applying what Jesus taught (Mat 28:19-20). This is what Jesus modeled by living with 12 men for 3 years. Making disciples through teaching and training in the midst of relationships is the objective! You can't do this during a traditional Sunday morning service only. Frankly, you could have a traditional or contemporary service every night of the week, and still not accomplish the objective of making disciples. It must be done within the context of daily living as Jesus taught us.

You can start by finding other believers who are on the same spiritual page as you are and begin meeting together in common sharing. Start thinking of simple ways to make friends with unbelievers. A key to multiplication in the kingdom of God is the flexibility to engage yourself in the lives of unbelievers outside the church and allow them to be a part of your life. In other words, develop a lifestyle with a relational focus on being a blessing to others. Be an example in your conduct and conversation, but don't neglect the preaching of the gospel and the power of God.

# CHAPTER 17

# The Restoration of Pentecost

Shortly after the day of Pentecost, Peter delivered a powerful word:

*"<u>Repent</u> therefore and be converted, that your sins may be blotted out, so that times of <u>refreshing</u> may come from the presence of the Lord, and that He may send Jesus Christ, who was preached to you before, whom heaven must receive until the times of <u>restoration</u> of all things, which God has spoken by the mouth of all His holy prophets since the world began"* (Acts 3:19-21).

True repentance should be followed by both times of refreshing and times of restoration that are promised to the Church, especially as the coming of the Lord draws nearer. Just before the Lord's coming we will experience both times of refreshing and the restoration of all things.

The coming restoration will be manifest in three primary areas in the Church: There will be a restoration of character, a restoration of power, and a restoration of authority. It is God's will to restore these three characteristics to the Church, both corporately and individually.

I wish to point out three aspects of true Pentecost that will bring forth and help give birth to this restoration. In other words, these three aspects are precursors of refreshing (revival), and the coming restoration.

The recovery of these aspects of Pentecost are so vital because many of our churches today are losing Pentecost as the early Church knew it and as the Holy Ghost designed it. We are living in a day when man's reputation has become more important than God's glory. Social status and education are more highly esteemed than the things of the Spirit.

When I asked 85 year old revivalist Hilton Sutton why we are not seeing more of a manifestation of the power of Pentecost he pointed to Western education as the greatest hindrance. He added that Europe and America are the biggest examples of this. Unsanctified intellect has robbed the Church of the power of God. Certainly education is important and to be esteemed, but we cannot afford to educate our intellect at the expense of our spirits. Our spirits must have the preeminence.

One foreign minister, who visited America, when asked what impressed him most about the American Church, replied: "How much she has been able to accomplish without God." We have conceded to natural means in our attempts to advance the kingdom of God. Showmanship and salesmanship seem to be at an all time high.

We must return to our roots. These three aspects will get us there.

## THE CROSS

The first aspect or precursor to the coming restoration is the message of the cross.

*"Beloved, while I was very diligent to write to you concerning our common salvation, I found it necessary to write to you exhorting you to contend earnestly for the faith which was once for all delivered to the saints"* (Jude 3).

The faith delivered to the saints was primarily the apostles teaching and foundation that was laid in the early Church. The first aspect of Pentecost that needs to be recovered from the apostolic doctrine is the message of the cross. The reason the Church in many places today is only a phantom of what it was 2,000 years ago is because the message of the cross is not preached nor lived. The fruit of this lack is that the distinction between the Church and the world is marred. It is difficult to tell them apart.

I believe the infiltration of humanism into the Church is the major cause of her departure from the true preaching of the cross. According to humanism in the Church, salvation is the pursuit of happiness in this life, and the gospel is used primarily as a means to improve our lifestyle. Let me ask a thought-provoking question: Are we guilty of modifying God's image and His Word to fit our happiness where God becomes only a means to an end? Have we created an image of God patterned more after the pop culture of our day than who the Scriptures declare Him to be? The pursuit of happiness is a godless philosophy that is a complete contradiction of the message of the cross, and a denial of the Lordship of Jesus Christ over our lives.

The Bible tells us to pursue holiness, not happiness (Heb 12:14). True happiness is a by-product of true holiness. It's not that God wants us sad and unhappy, but that our decisions should be based on His will and not our own personal safety, personal comfort, personal convenience, and personal happiness. When we return to the message of the cross we will see a restoration of the character of Christ in the Church. We will see true holiness and sanctification become a normal part of the daily lives of many more Christians. We desperately need to return to the preaching of the cross and living the life of the cross.

## PRAYER AND INTERCESSION

The second aspect or precursor to the coming restoration is prayer and intercession which also includes waiting on the Lord.

One of my spiritual fathers Kenneth Hagin said that the Lord told him that there are some areas of prayer and intercession that will be lost unless those who are experienced in prayer get those truths over to this present generation. There is a realm of prayer and deep intercession that most believers today know nothing about. If God's plans and purposes are to be fulfilled in this hour, and if we are to see the restoration of the power and authority of Christ in the Church, more and more believers need to learn to pray this way. For example, travail is almost a lost art in the Church. The same could be said about praying in other tongues. Even among Pentecostals and Spirit-baptized people, recent statistics reveal that only 15% of them use their prayer language on a regular basis.

God needs skilled intercessors in this hour. He needs people who are sensitive to the realm of the Spirit and receptive to his gentle promptings. And you can't cultivate that without spending much time praying in other tongues.

Years ago in Bible school a praying man named Phil Halverson was called to the platform to pray. When he opened his mouth it was obvious that he possessed a spirit of prayer unlike most of us had ever witnessed before. When Brother Halverson prayed the heavens opened and nearly everyone fell to their knees in that auditorium and began to pray. I had never witnessed someone agonize in prayer until that day. It sounded as if Brother Halverson was going to die as he prayed from the very depths of the heart of God. Students were overcome by a spirit of prayer. No one could even engage in conversation afterwards.

Skilled intercessors understand the art of travail. They are often awakened in the nighttime and are familiar with what I call "spiritual alerts." In other words, because they live near to God's presence, they know when someone's life is in danger, or when someone desperately needs God's help and intervention in some area. They know if it is a lost person they are praying for or a coming demonic attack that must be stopped. You don't cultivate that kind of sensitivity or familiarity with the Spirit overnight.

## WAITING ON THE LORD

Ministering to the Lord in supernatural utterances in psalms, hymns, and spiritual songs has also become a lost art. Many are not even familiar with this realm. Much of our singing in churches is not patterned according to these supernatural utterances, but only from a song book. The Church today really knows so little about speaking or singing to ourselves or to one another in psalms, hymns, and spiritual songs. I've been in full gospel churches where singing in the Spirit is no longer encouraged or even allowed. It has become foreign to some Pentecostal believers. And yet it was common to the early Church (Eph 5:18-19; Col 3:16; Jam 5:13). Undoubtedly. there is a diminishing ability in the body of Christ to draw from the Spirit of God in deep prayer, in making true spiritual intercession, and in ministering to the Lord in these supernatural utterances.

The old Pentecostals used to have "tarrying" meetings where they would wait to receive the Holy Spirit. Once they received the Holy Spirit, though, they stopped "tarrying." What they should've done was to tarry or "wait" on God after they received the Holy Spirit. Tarrying simply means to wait on God and minister to Him either corporately as a body of believers, or in one's individual prayer life. Waiting on the Lord causes renewal and refreshing in your spirit. That is what the early disciples were doing in the upper room before the power of the Holy Spirit was released, and they continued the practice throughout the days of the early Church (Acts 4:23-31; Acts 13:1-3). Waiting on the Lord is another aspect of prayer and true Pentecost the Church needs to recover today.

*"I've often thought that if I ever pastor another church, I would have regular prayer 'waiting' meetings."* Kenneth E. Hagin

Kenneth Hagin went on to say that if we had more of these kinds of meetings most believers wouldn't need any counseling because they'd get their answer from waiting on God. The Lord also told him that most Christians don't need any counseling anyway. "What they need to do is pray through," he said.

## FASTING

A final aspect or precursor to the coming restoration is fasting.

*"Moreover, when you fast..."* (Mat 6:16-17).

*"But the days will come when the Bridegroom will be taken away from them; then they will fast in those days"* (Lk 5:35).

*"This kind does not go out except by prayer and fasting"* (Mat 17:20).

*"As they ministered to the Lord and fasted, the Holy Spirit said..."* (Acts 13:2).

Here is yet another lost art in the Church today. Prayer with fasting has been called the master key to the impossible.

It was fasting that played an instrumental part in the most important conversion in the early Church. Immediately after the apostle Paul's radical encounter with the Lord Jesus Christ he ate no food nor drank water for three full days (Acts 9:9). The result was that a certain disciple named Ananias was sent to him with heaven's instructions and deliverance. Paul's life was forever changed. Who's to say if this supernatural communication and vision would've ever been unveiled to both Ananias and Paul had not Paul waited on God in fasting and praying?

It was also fasting and praying that positioned Cornelius to receive a visitation from heaven that opened a great door of the gospel to the Gentiles (Acts 10). Think of the future impact on the Gentile world of this one visitation.

It was fasting and praying that allowed Paul and Barnabas to be separated and sent with great power to the Gentiles as the first ever missionaries (Acts 13:1-4a). Think again of the impact of this Holy Spirit initiated direction.

Adding fasting to prayer puts you in a position to not only be purged of your own inabilities and infirmities, but to receive faith for operations of the Spirit. Fasting and prayer blocks Satan where he has no accessibility to your life because when you shut the flesh down you shut down Satan. It is the flesh nature Satan uses to gain entry into your life. A lifestyle of prayer and fasting is what Jesus wants for His people. This is the primary way the operation of the flesh will eventually drop below the operation of the Spirit in your life where manifestations to your prayers come quicker, and you qualify for the highest calling in your life because of the character transformation that will take place in you.

One day I was reading from 2 Kings 2 where Elijah was taken up by a whirlwind to heaven. Elisha, who was following closely, was separated from Elijah, and took hold of his own clothes and tore them in two pieces. Then he picked up Elijah's mantle; the mantle signifying the power and anointing of God. When I was meditating on this glorious account it seemed like the Spirit of God asked me a question. "How do you pick up the mantle?" The answer came: "It is through prayer and fasting!" The restoration of true Pentecost will not happen without the vital aspect of prayer with fasting.

## CONCLUSION: PRAYER, FASTING, AND THE CROSS

At the end of Jesus' ministry and time on the earth, before the power of Pentecost was released in the early Church, Jesus made three stops. First, He went to the garden of Gethsemane. Secondly, He went to the scourging post. And thirdly He carried His cross to Golgotha's hill before being crucified on it.

At the garden Jesus went into deep agonizing *prayer* (Mat 26:36-42). At the scourging post His flesh was subjected to heavy flogging and beatings (John 19:1). This is symbolic of the life of *fasting*. And finally Jesus took up His *cross* and carried it (John 19:17). Even though Jesus lived a life of prayer and fasting and self-denial (cross-bearing), it was at the end of His life and ministry in the hour of His greatest trial that He exemplified these aspects to their greatest measure. Ultimately it was these three aspects in cooperation with the Spirit of God that defeated the flesh, the world, and the devil and purchased eternal redemption for us. And it was these three aspects that finally brought Pentecost to the Church.

This is the same journey we must be on. This is the same pattern that must be established in the Church of today. Preach and live the cross. Cultivate a life of prayer and fasting. When more and more believers do this, there will be a restoration of the character, the power, and the authority of Christ in the Church. The glory of God will manifest and a harvest of souls shall be reaped!

# CHAPTER 18

# What is True Revival?

Revival is not the pursuit of any manifestation or aspect of ministry whether it be miracles, signs, wonders, visions, shaking, trembling, falling down, weeping, laughter, healing, deliverance, appearances of gold dust, and anything else you could possibly hear of. Most of these kinds of manifestations are frequent in times of revival, but they are not the revival. They may accompany revival or lead to revival, but they are not necessarily evidence of revival.

Revival is a definite outpouring of the Holy Spirit on the Church and then those she is called to reach.

Revival is a restoration of Divine life from deadness and dullness. It is a return to spiritual health, vibrancy, and vigor.

Revival awakens us from a sleeping heart and stirs us from our slumber. We become conscious of heaven and of eternal things.

Revival means to flourish after a time of decline; to come back into use; to become valid, effective, and operative again.

Revival is when the saints return to normal, when the Holy Spirit becomes their oxygen, when a hunger to know God is the norm, when being conformed to His image is their focus, when evangelism and discipleship become a lifestyle.

The primary purpose of revival is not initially for the enjoyment of the Church but for her cleansing, renewal, and refreshing. A cleansed, renewed, and refreshed Church in the hands of God will do the most good.

I believe one of the final moves of God's Spirit on the earth will be to ignite His people with an intense, burning passion for God that will yield true holiness and prepare it for the glory and harvest to come, as well as the Lord's soon return. It is only a revived Church that will accomplish the full purposes of God.

Charles Finney defined revival as, *"A renewed conviction of sin and repentance followed by an intense desire to live in obedience to God."* It is only under the influence of the Holy Spirit that conviction and repentance are birthed. God, working through the preaching of men (Acts 20:21), commands people everywhere to repent (Acts 17:30), and then grants repentance as a gift (Acts 11:18).

There is always a man-ward part and a God-ward part in the promotion of revival. **"One plants, another waters, but it is God that brings the increase"** (1 Cor 3:6-7). A farmer prepares his field, plants seed, and waters that seed, but sown seed is no guarantee of a harvest without God's blessing on the laws of nature. Just as a good farmer has tools to produce a harvest so praying, preaching, and the power of God are tools God has given us as a means to revival. However, it still takes God's grace and blessing to produce it.

For example, in the wilderness journeys of Israel when the waters of Marah had become bitter God told Moses to cast the tree into the waters. When he did, the waters were made sweet (Ex 15:22-25). So what or who caused the sweetness? Was it the tree or was it Moses? It was neither. Actually, it was God's power that did it, and the obedience of Moses triggered it.

It is human nature to attempt to imitate revivals of the past or depend on some blueprint or strategy that worked in the past. We should endeavor not to do that, but instead put our dependence on God. Our part is to simply obey the written Word and what the Spirit of God is saying to us and use the tools and means God has given us. If we do this we can expect revival.

Methods and men cannot produce revival without the Holy Spirit's orchestration. There are two extremes here: The first being that some people work in their own strength trying to produce revival through imitation, hype, or programs of one kind or another. The second extreme is that some wait endlessly for what they refer to as "the sovereignty of God" to bring revival. Neither is correct. No doctrine endangers the Church more than this last extreme.

## WHAT HAPPENS IN A REVIVAL

The greatest fruit of a true revival is when backsliders and sinners are delivered from their sinful practices and begin to conform to Christ. The first work of the Spirit is not to tell people how to be happy but how to be holy. As stated above, revival begins with the conviction of sin; conviction that people can feel, conviction that hurts, and finally a conviction that culminates in repentance and then obedience.

My first introduction to the Pensacola outpouring (1995–2000) that lasted nearly five years was a deep conviction of sin and people weeping and wailing over their sins. Even the elementary age children could be heard in one service moaning and groaning with a consciousness of sin and an acute awareness of the lost condition of mankind. Uncontrollable weeping, trembling, confession of sin, and united prayer marked many of the services. People came from nearly every state in America and around the world and would stand in line from early morning until evening to attend the services. Man cannot produce that kind of overwhelming response and expectation from the people by putting a sign out in front of the church building advertising the services, or by devising human methods to promote revival.

In one meeting large trash bins were placed on the altar and many who were turning from their sins came forward and threw away what the evangelist called, "articles of affection." Drug paraphernalia, marijuana, cigarettes, condoms, pornographic magazines, and the like were carried forward by many in tears and discarded once and for all. When their repentance culminated with this type of action then their tears of godly sorrow would turn into tears of wonderful joy. "Blessed are those who mourn." That is a picture of what happens in true revival.

Revival throws light in the dark places of our lives. It removes deception and deals with attitudes of our hearts the naked eye cannot see. In revival people weep over sins they once entertained.

Revival results in a thorough removal of sinful practices, like the grinding to powder of Aaron's golden calf (Num 32); like King Josiah's crushing of the pagan altars and then scattering them into the Kidron Valley (2 Kings 23); like the burning of the magic books in Ephesus

(Acts 19). True revival offers no compromise with the devil, the flesh, and sin. It reserves mercy only for the truly repentant and gives grace to help the needy. One cannot read the story of the revivals of old without understanding this. There is no honor to God in a revival that does not produce the fruits of holiness.

When revival comes our priorities change. Pleasing God becomes more important than pleasing ourselves. Sin and doubtful habits begin to trouble us. The fear of God is restored in us, and there is a wonderful cleansing from all sin and a fresh infilling of the Spirit of God.

In revival the fire of God burns away the roots of sin and molds our hearts to God's heart. It purifies our motives and ignites us to action.

Holiness is the one outstanding mark of revival. If a so-called revival does not produce the fruits of holiness then it is not true revival. If there is not lasting change in the lives of the people then it is not the real thing. If it does not alter our appetites and passions and give us a greater hunger for God and for Biblical holiness then it is not fulfilling the purposes of God regardless of how many people attend and how much excitement it generates.

Duncan Campbell, who experienced the glory of God in extraordinary ways in the Hebrides revival off the coast of Scotland (from 1949–1952), said: *"Revival is always a revival of holiness."*

When you have renewal and refreshing without fundamental repentance and obedience, you quickly return to your old ways once the experience wanes. You get touched by God, you get excited, but a few days later you are the same. If your encounters with the Lord don't lead you into a deeper fellowship with Him, into the Word and prayer, and a greater life transformation then all you got was a skin-deep experience.

Understand that revival does not begin with the glory. Revival does not usually begin with the joy of the Lord. Instead, it often begins with holy conviction, sometimes with tears, and always accompanied by godly sorrow. Revival then culminates with the continued manifestation of the presence of God that aligns our hearts and lives with the Father's will.

In effect, 5 of the 7 letters written to the churches in Revelation were with an emphasis on repentance so these churches could be revived. Repentance is usually a precursor to revival. Blessing and reward was promised on the truly repentant churches of Revelation, but a certain judgment was declared on those who refused change.

The God who allowed the judgment of Ananias and Sapphira (Acts 5) is the same God today. The God who judged Uzzah (2 Sam 6) is the same God today. The God who judged Achan (Joshua 7), and before him Nadab and Abihu (Lev 10), is still as holy now as He was then. Remember, without holiness no man shall see the Lord (Heb 12:14).

Revival fire creates a hunger for God and for prayer which is the basis and foundation of revival. A church that is consumed with a spirit of prayer is a church in revival. Once the operation of the flesh drops below the operation of the spirit, when spiritual activity supersedes fleshly activity, you are experiencing revival and what is considered normal Christianity. Revival wanes when the opposite happens and this process is reversed.

*"Let Christians in a revival beware, when they first find an inclination creeping upon them to shrink from self-denial, and to give in to one self-indulgence after another. It is the device of Satan to 'bait' them off from the work of God, and make them dull and gross, lazy and fearful, useless and sensual; and so drive away the Spirit and destroy the revival."*
Charles Finney

**"Will You not revive us again, that Your people may rejoice in You"**
**(Ps 85:6).**

# CHAPTER 19

# Where is the Awesome Holiness and Irresistible Power of God?

We are missing something in this generation. A carnality, a casualness, and a complacency have left us void of the reality of God's mighty power and holy presence. A party spirit, a prayer-less posture, pomp and pride has hindered the Spirit's manifestations.

The Church has created a smokescreen that has hidden her true spiritual condition. Our big ornate buildings, our popular conventions and conferences, the Hollywood glare that so many of today's ministers bask in, the noise of our promotions and advertisements make it painfully clear that the fame of men is greater than the fame of the Master.

Match that up against these mighty workings of God in years gone by.

A wind blew through the building and in an instant every sinner and backslider came to God, every sick person was healed, and everyone was filled with the Holy Spirit.

A light bulb flash went off in the church building. Everyone saw it. Suddenly several people were down at the altar. No one knew how they got there. It was evident that they were trans-located by an act of God.

A cloud rolled into the meeting place. As soon as it did everyone fell on their faces and began to pray.

A lady praised the Lord and danced right off the platform into mid-air and stayed there for a few seconds and continued dancing.

History records that within 50 miles of Maria-Woodworth Etter's meetings people fell under the power and became stiff as boards. They would then have to be carried to the meeting to be touched and loosed. Many of them would have visions of heaven and hell, and they would fall to the ground under tremendous conviction. It was like a "blanket" anointing that covered the entire area and in whole blocks around her meetings people were falling to the ground and repenting.

In one meeting in 1936 at Shepherds Hill outside Louisville, KY hundreds of people were genuinely slain in the Spirit laying all over the area outside. The bread-man drove up and saw hundreds weeping, others speaking in tongues, others still and prostrate, while yet others were rolling crying out to God. The bread-man turned around and drove down as fast as he could.

At times in past revivals the manifested presence of God created what some have termed as a divine radiation zone, and everyone coming within its reach of power is brought under intense conviction.

During the 1857 revival for example, ships entered into a definite zone of the convicting influence of the presence of God as they drew near port. Ship after ship arrived with reports of sudden conviction and conversion among the crew members. This sort of conviction is the most outstanding feature of revival.

Historic accounts tell us that Charles Finney's prayer partner, Father Daniel Nash, would go into an area a couple of weeks ahead of Finney and find one or two other mature praying saints and begin to pray and travail for lost souls. As it has been recorded, the way they knew the time was ready to summon Finney was that they looked out the window in the day when many were on the streets, and when men began falling to their knees in holy conviction Finney was called. Who has heard of such a thing in our day?

Just one glance or look from historic revival giants like Smith Wigglesworth and Charles Finney would convict sinners of their sin.

Not only did men of old manifest Christ through their eyes, but they also kept their tongues under the power of God as they spoke forth the revelation of the Spirit through divinely inspired utterances that shot through people like lightning.

Other times, preachers, like prophets of old were struck dumb by the Spirit and couldn't speak at all.

George Whitfield preached in the open air in Boston where thousands would gather. Youth would climb trees to better see and hear the preacher. He would tell them to come down so they would not fall and get injured when the power of God would start moving. Without Whitfield or anyone laying hands on people they fell under the power of God all over the grounds.

There have been historic accounts of people falling into a trance with their physical senses suspended as they stood frozen like a statue for hours or even days. Multitudes would come from miles around to see it. It was a sign and a wonder of God's power in manifestation.

In the Bible men like Peter and Paul experienced trances.

Visions and dreams were given.

Saul, one of the greatest persecutors of the Church saw a glorious blinding light, was knocked off his high horse, blinded for 3 days, and became one of the greatest apostles to ever live, writing a large portion of the New Testament.

Throughout Church history and past revivals not only did men often shake under the power of God, but in the beginnings of the Church age buildings shook.

Divine earthquakes opened prison doors and loosed prisoners from their chains.

A couple was struck dead in a church meeting for lying to the Holy Ghost.

A man was struck blind for trying to hinder the gospel.

The dead were raised.

Angels appeared.

Miracles of healing and deliverance were common.

Here is a recent testimony from a dialogue I had with a friend that speaks of not only the powerful moves of the Spirit in days of old but of the Word they preached.

*"The men and women of old knew nothing of the extensiveness of error in the cotton candy gospel of today. They nipped it in the bud. They stated without apology that without holiness we won't see the Lord. They knew scripture far better than today's Bible professors. Sister Pauline Parham, the daughter-in-law of Charles Parham, told me in Dallas in the early 80s that the old preachers knew the Word far better than the new generation, and powerful moves of the Spirit not seen today were common."*

Why aren't we seeing this kind of aforementioned power and un-usual signs and wonders in and through the Church today? For one, we are not preaching the real gospel and the vital themes of the New Testament. God confirms His gospel and His Word. Isn't it interesting that the top three television preachers in America no longer men-tion the cross, the blood, and hell in their preaching? That is the first time this has happened in American history. And the theme of repen-tance is clearly absent.

Earlier in this book I referred to a word the Lord gave a certain prophet when he was inquiring of the reason more Christians are sick today than when he first started in ministry decades ago. He told the Lord that we have so much more light and knowledge of healing today. There is an abundance of faith building resources from audio, to video, to the written page concerning our healing covenant that we did not have decades ago. And yet there are more Christians sick today than during that time. Why? The Lord responded by saying, "Yes, and they were more consecrated, too." And so there you have it. Consecration was the key to more Christians walking in divine health.

I believe the second reason we are not seeing the power of God in manifestation in a great measure is due to this lack of consecration and Holy Spirit filled prayer.

At this critical point and juncture in our nation the awesome revelation of the holiness of God and His irresistible power is the only thing that will change it and alter its course.

# CHAPTER 20

# Prophecies and Visions from Yesterday That Warn Us Today

(These visions and prophecies are public domain and have been widely circulated and shared on many sites. Feel free to trace their origin and to share them as well. It is obvious that many of the things that were seen and prophesied in these visions have already come to pass. We are alerted, awakened, and encouraged by such things to live in peace, without spot and blameless, looking for and hastening the Day of God. [2 Peter 3:14])

## VISION #1: ASTONISHING 1968 PROPHECY BY 90 YEAR OLD WOMAN

An old woman of 90 from Valdres in Norway had a vision from God in 1968. The evangelist Emanuel Minos had meetings (services) where she lived. He had the opportunity to meet her, and she told him what she had seen. He wrote it down, but thought it to be so unintelligible that he put it in a drawer. Then nearly 30 years later he understood it and began sharing her vision with others.

The woman from Valdres was a very alert, reliable, awake and credible Christian, with a good reputation among all who knew her. This is what she saw:

"I saw the time just before the coming of Jesus and the outbreak of the Third World War. I saw the events with my natural eyes. I saw the world like a kind of a globe and saw Europe, land by land. I saw Scandinavia. I saw Norway. I saw certain things that would take place just before the return of Jesus, and just before the last calamity happens, a calamity the likes of which we have never before experienced.

She mentioned four waves:

**1. "First, before Jesus comes and before the Third World War breaks out there will be a 'détente' like we have never had before.** There will be peace between the super powers in the east and the west, and there will be a long peace. (Remember, that this was in 1968 when the cold war was at its highest. E. Minos). In this period of peace there will be disarmament in many countries, also in Norway, and we are not prepared when it (the war) comes. The Third World War will begin in a way no one would have anticipated—and from an unexpected place.

**2. "A lukewarmness without parallel will take hold of the Christians, a falling away from true, living Christianity.** Christians will not be open for penetrating preaching. They will not, like in earlier times, want to hear of sin and grace, law and gospel, repentance and restoration. There will come a substitute instead: prosperity (happiness) Christianity.

"The important thing will be to have success, to be something; to have material things, things that God never promised us in this way.

Churches and prayer houses will be emptier and emptier. Instead of the preaching we have been used to for generations—like, to take your cross up and follow Jesus—entertainment, art and culture will invade the churches where there should have been gatherings for repentance and revival. This will increase markedly just before the return of Jesus.

**3. "There will be a moral disintegration that old Norway has never experienced the likes of.** People will live together like married without being married. (I do not believe the concept of 'co-habitation' existed in 1968—E. Minos.) Much uncleanness before marriage, and much infidelity in marriage will become the natural (the common), and it will be justified from every angle. It will even enter Christian circles and we pet it—even sin against nature (homosexuality and lesbianism). Just before Jesus returns there will be TV programs like we have never experienced. (TV had just arrived in Norway in 1968. E. Minos)

"TV will be filled with such horrible violence that it teaches people to murder and destroy each other, and it will be unsafe in our streets. People will copy what they see. There will not be only one 'station' on TV; it will be filled with 'stations.' (She did not know the word 'channel' which we use today. Therefore she called them stations. E. Minos.) TV will be just like the radio where we have many stations and it will be filled with violence. People will use it for entertainment. We will see terrible scenes of murder and destruction of one another, and this will spread in society. Sex scenes will also be shown on the screen, the most intimate things that takes place in a marriage." (I protested and said we have a paragraph that forbids this kind of thing. E. Minos.) There the old woman said: "It will happen, and you will see it. All we have had before will be broken down, and the most indecent things will pass before our eyes.

**4. "People from poor countries will stream to Europe.** (In 1968 there was no such thing as immigration. E. Minos.) They will also come to Scandinavia—and Norway. There will be so many of them that people will begin to dislike them and become hard with them. They will be treated like the Jews before the Second World War. Then the full measure of our sins will have been reached (I protested at the issue of immigration. I did not understand it at the time. E. Minos.)

The tears streamed from the old woman's eyes down her cheeks. "I will not see it, but you will. Then suddenly, Jesus will come and the Third World War breaks out. It will be a short war." (She saw it in the vision.)

"All that I have seen of war before is only child's play compared to this one, and it will be ended with a nuclear atom bomb. The air will be so polluted that one cannot draw one's breath. It will cover several continents, America, Japan, Australia and the wealthy nations. The water will be ruined (contaminated). We can no longer till the soil. The result will be that only a remnant will remain. The remnant in the wealthy countries will try to flee to the poor countries, but they will be as hard on us as we were on them.

"I am so glad that I will not see it, but when the time draws near, you must take courage and tell this. I have received it from God, and nothing of it goes against what the Bible tells.

"The one who has his sin forgiven and has Jesus as Savior and Lord, is safe."

# VISION #2: A SATAN AND A GOD REVIVAL

The following is an end time vision given to an established, seasoned minister of the gospel and told in his own words. My heart was quickened when I read it and I thought: "This vision needs to be circulated to the body of Christ worldwide for we are seeing the increasing effects of it being unfolded in this hour, although it was given more than 25 years ago."

If you are skeptical of these things I would encourage you to listen to your heart as you read it and allow the Holy Spirit to bear witness with you.

*But you have an anointing from the Holy One, and you know all things.*

*But the anointing which you have received from Him abides in you, and you do not need that anyone teach you; but as the same anointing teaches you concerning all things, and is true, and is not a lie, and just as it has taught you, you will abide in Him.* (1 John 2:20, 27)

Here then is the vision told in the minister's own words:

"In 1987, I was a speaker at a camp meeting in Tulsa, Oklahoma. I spoke during the Thursday evening service. Dr. Kenneth E. Hagin spoke during the Friday evening service. I remember that I had just flown in from meetings in Paris, France. I mentioned to my wife how much I would like to stay and hear Dr. Hagin speak. She agreed.

As Dr. Hagin entered the pulpit, he began to pray in tongues. When he started, I started. A moment later, I was caught up in a vision

(I was told later that it was probably more like a trance). As I went into this vision, I remember how Dr. Hagin's voice was getting quieter and quieter, until I could hear him no more. It was so quiet all around me I felt like I could hear my own heartbeat.

All of a sudden I felt evil, as if it were surrounding me. Anger rose up in me, and fear tried to get a grip on me. Suddenly, something caught my attention out of my left eye. I turned hard to the left to see what it was. I saw the circumference of the earth, from one edge to the other, and this horrible black, dark cloud was rising up over the horizon. Somehow I knew it would eventually fill the entire earth.

An alarm went off in me, screaming to me to run away from it as fast as I could. I felt like I should scream at it, to stop it in its tracks by using the name of Jesus.

I began to rebuke it and started to say, "In the name of Jesus. . ." I didn't quite get it out, and the Lord said, "That will do you no good."

"What?" I said.

The Lord said, "Son, you cannot use My name to stop what I prophesied. I am not causing this dark cloud, but I did prophesy it would happen in the last days."

I remember in the vision that I asked the Lord "What is this? What is this evil, tempestuous dark cloud?"

The Lord said, "This is what I showed My prophet, Isaiah (Isaiah 61: 1-2). This is every evil thing you can name. It is every demon, it is every disease, and it is sickness and bacterial attacks that haven't even been discovered yet. It will cause humans to do things to humans that aren't even human. It is filled with insanity, and many people will lose their mind and their faculties. It is murder, terror, rape, abuse, terrorism, torture, and much worse. It is filled with deceptions, heresies, perversions, and filth."

Some things the Lord showed me I have not had permission to speak.

I also saw people—many, many people. Some were running into the dark cloud, and some were being sucked into it. It reminded me of this very powerful Shop-vac I have. It will not only suck up the dirt but also my tools, if I don't pay attention.

I saw many people screaming with terror and actually being dragged into this cloud. Though they were refusing it and resisting it with all their strength, they still did not possess the power to stop it.

I was so disturbed when I saw a cross on someone's pocket or jewelry. I remember saying to the Lord, "Who are those people being drawn into this filth and terror, wearing the Christian symbol of the cross? Who are these people, not even resisting? And who are these people, resisting with all their might but it does them no good? They just keep disappearing into this horrible, evil cloud of gross darkness."

The Lord answered me and said, "Oh, these are those who do not have clean hands and a pure heart. They have been warned but ignored the warnings. Some even wanted this filth as their lifestyle."

I asked, "Well, who are these wearing the cross?"

"Oh," the Lord said, "These are the people who claim Me as Savior. Many of them have desired this filth and even fought for it. They make excuses but are not excused. The ones who are resisting thought My prophets were exaggerating and from the old school, and they denied the warnings. Now that this evil has come, they possess little to no power, and certainly not enough to resist and overcome this horrible onslaught of enemy power. Only those with clean hands and a pure heart will be able to totally resist this. It will cover the earth."

There was much more to this, but I began to come out of the vision and once again heard Brother Hagin speaking in tongues from the pulpit.

I asked my wife what had happened, and she said, "Nothing, he hasn't done anything but pray in the spirit."

I began to realize that nobody seemed to see this vision or get caught up into this trance but me. I held my wife's hand a little tighter and began to pray fervently in the spirit. As I did, I got caught up in the spirit again.

Just like before, Brother Hagin's voice got quieter and quieter until it was gone. I found myself alone again. It was so quiet I could hear my own heartbeat. Suddenly, a piercing light hit the corner of my right eye. It was so bright that I instantly shrouded my head with my hands and arms. It reminded me of the intense light that my optometrist uses to examine the back of my eyes. Actually, it was much brighter than that.

Everything within me said, "Turn, and look into it. Turn now, and run into it." Yet there was this hesitation because it was so bright it seemed to shine through me. Finally I gave in to it and looked directly at it. With both eyes I saw the depth of this bright cloud. Just like the dark cloud I had seen before, it was coming up over the horizon of the earth. I could tell that it was going to cover the planet. I just knew that I knew that nothing could stop it.

I remembered asking the Lord, "What is this? What is this massive, earth-consuming bright cloud?"

The Lord answered me and said, "Oh, this is My glory. This is the glory cloud that I showed My prophet Isaiah (Isa. 61:1-2). This is what I promised, that My glory will fill the whole earth."

"Well," I asked, "what is inside the cloud?"

"It is filled with the greatest miracles humans have ever seen. It is filled with healing for every disease, and a cure for every sickness. It is power to overcome sin and filth—to receive the truth and reject error, heresy, and doctrines of demons. It is a full manifestation of My Spirit. It is the full anointing of Jesus Christ and more, much more."

He showed me other things that I have no permission to speak at this time.

I saw people in this vision, just like before with the cloud of darkness. Many, many people were running into it and almost frolicking in it. It was like my first response—too bright to behold, and then I wanted to run into it. There were those who seemed to want to pull away from this glory cloud.

"Lord, who will enter into this great glory of God and enjoy this awesome power?" I asked.

"Those who have a pure heart and clean hands," the Lord answered. "They are the ones who will escape the horrible vacuum of the evil, dark cloud and be consumed with my glory. I will require you to tell these things to My people at an appointed time."

Now is that time! As I travel the world over, I see both of these manifestations happening. In fact, I see them beginning to intensify. Sometimes I say that both God and Satan are having a revival among men. We will now see more and more people running to each cloud, causing a great gulf or divide. Could this be the separation of sheep and goats, or the separation of wheat and tares?

I am not a conspiracy-theory person. I am not a fear-based preacher. I am not a prophet of doom. So what I am about to say is none of these. But, I am actually witnessing the spirits of the antichrist, prepping the people of the earth (including many church goers) for the arrival of the antichrist himself. I see demons (spirits of the antichrist) going throughout all the earth. They are slowly re-programming the minds of men (doctrines of demons) to systematically disassemble the work of Christ and disengage the army of God.

You can avoid this, if you choose. If you choose not to, you will suffer the consequences. Please don't do that!" Dr. Mark Barclay

## PROPHECY #1: AMAZING 1927 SMITH WIGGLESWORTH MESSAGE

On August 11, 1927, Smith Wigglesworth stood in Angelus Temple to preach on preparing for the Second Coming of Christ. He told the audience that liquid fire was consuming him. Then Wigglesworth made this opening statement:

But there will be things that will happen prior to His coming that we shall know. You can tell. I am like one this morning that is moving with a liquid, holy, indispensable, real fire in my bosom, and I know it is burning and the body is not consumed. It is real fire from heaven that is making my utterances come to you to know that He is coming. He is on the way. God is going to help me tell you why you will know. You that have the breath of the Spirit, there is something now moving as I speak. As I speak, this breath of mighty, quickening, moving, changing, desirable power is making you know and it is this alone that is making you know that you will be ready.

1. **There must be special preparation for the return of Christ and at least half of all believers will be totally unprepared**. We have to see that these days have to come before the Lord can come. There has to be a falling away. I want to speak to you very exactly. All the people which are pressing into and getting ready for this glorious attained place where they shall not be found naked, where they shall be blameless, where they shall be immovable, where they shall be purified by the power of the Word of God, have within them a consciousness of the very presence of God within, changing their very nature and preparing them for a greater thing, and causing them to be ready for translation.

This is the day of purifying. This is the day of holiness. This is the day of separation. This is the day of waking. O God let us wake today! Let the inner spirit wake into consciousness that God is calling us. *There are in the world two classes of believers. There are believers which are disobedient, or I ought to say there are children which are saved by the power of God which are disobedient children. And there are children which are just the same saved by the power of God who all the time are longing to be more obedient.*

And we heard the word come rushing, through all over, "new theology" that damnable, devilish, evil power that lived in some of these disobedient children, which in these last days opened the door to the next thing.

**2. There will be many Christians who believe that they can do whatever they want and God will look the other way.** People are tremendously afraid of this position because they have heard so much on this line: "Oh, you know you are the elect of God. You are sure to be all right." There have been in England great churches which were laid out upon these things. I thank God that they're all withered. You will find if you go to England those strong people that used to hold all these things are almost withered out. Why? Because they went on to say whatever you did, if you were elect, you were right. That is wrong. The elect of God are those that are pressing forward.

**3. It will be common for preachers to deny the existence of hell.** Denying hell prepares the way for antichrist. What? No hell. The devil has always said that "what does Christian Science say?" No hell, no devil. They are ready for him. The devil has always said no hell, no evil. (Movements such as Universalism, the false ecumenical movement, with such things as Crislam, the joining of Islam and Christianity, and some of the cults like Jehovah's Witnesses deny the existence of hell.) These people are preparing, and even though they do not realize it, for the Man of Sin.

**4. It is offensive to talk about the blood of Christ.** When I spoke about the blood and when I spoke about this infernal thing, the whole place was upset. ***You be careful when anybody comes to you with a sugar-coated pill or with a slimy tongue. They are always of the devil.***

The Spirit of the Lord will always deal with truth. These people never deal with truth. They always cover up the truth.

Do you believe it? Who can do it? THE BLOOD CAN DO IT! The blood, the blood, Oh the blood! The blood of the Lamb. The blood of Jesus can do it. Spotless, clean, preserved for God. Give the devil the biggest chase of his life and say these words: "The blood of Jesus Christ, God's Son, cleanses us from all unrighteousness."

**5. The world will look to worship a man and will overlook his faults to get him into power. These people are determined to have a man.** They know someone has to come. We know Who He is that is coming. They begin to make a man. So they find a man in India, they polish him up as much as they can, and they make him as—well, in appearance, but you know we are told by the Lord that there is soft clothing that goes onto wolves' backs.

**6. That people believe that certain preachers are of God simply because of their crowds and their buildings.** A person said to me, "You see, the Christian Scientists must be right—look at the beautiful buildings. Look at all the people following them." Yes, everybody can belong to it. You can go to any brother you like, you can go to any theater you like, you can go to any race course you like, you can be mixed up with the rest of the people in your life and still be a Christian Scientist. You can have the devil right and left and anywhere, and still belong to Christian Science.

**7. As Churches turn away from the Holy Spirit many believers go to false teachers.** The secret of many people going into Christian Science is a barren church that had not the Holy Ghost. Christian Science exists because the churches have a barren place because they haven't the Holy Ghost. There would be no room for Christian Science if the churches were filled with the Holy Ghost.

**8. The last days are a time for the true people of God to engage in extravagant asking.** Up to this present time, the Lord's word is for us, "Hitherto ye have asked nothing." Surely you people that have been asking great things from God for a long time would be amazed if you entered into it with clear knowledge that it is the Master, it is Jesus, who has such knowledge of the mightiness of the power of the Father, of the joint union with Him, that nothing is impossible for you to ask. Surely it is He only Who could say, "Hitherto you have asked nothing." So God means me to press you another step forward. Begin to believe on extravagant asking, believing that God is pleased when you ask large things.

## PROPHECY #2: 1965 PROPHECY BY STANLEY FRODSHAM

(NOTE: This prophetic word was spoken by Prophet Stanley Frodsham who was a personal friend of Smith Wigglesworth, a traveling companion and author of one of the books about Him. It was given in Chicago in 1965, five years before he died.)

## GREAT JUDGMENTS

"With great judgments will I plead with the population of this country. Great darkness is coming upon the countries that have heard My gospel but no longer walk in it. My wrath shall come upon them. The darkness shall be so great and the anguish so sore that men shall cry out for death and shall not find it. There shall be a lingering death, famine and great catastrophes.

My wrath shall be manifested against all ungodliness. It shall come with great intensity. You have known My love but have not experienced My wrath or My severity. My judgments are literal and not a thing to be passed over lightly. Realize the severity of My judgments and My intense anger against the sin in My household. My judgments shall begin in My house, for I will cleanse My house that it be not a partaker of My wrath against the iniquities of the cities. Before I visit the nations in judgment; I will begin at My house. When I do cause My wrath to come upon the cities of the world, My people shall be separate. I desire a people without spot or wrinkle and such will be preserved by Me in the time of My wrath, which will be coming upon all iniquity and unrighteousness.

I am going to prepare you for the coming days by a hard path that will cause many to cry out continually unto Me. For when the going is easy men do not seek Me, but rejoice in a temporary blessing. And when that blessing is removed they so often turn this way and that way but do not come to Me. I am showing you these things in order that you may seek Me continually and with great diligence. As you seek Me I will open up truths to you that you have not seen before, and these very truths will be such that will enable you to stand in these last days. As you are persecuted, reviled and rejected by your brethren then you will turn unto Me with all your heart and seek Me for that spiritual life that you need. So that when the tribulation comes you will have that which will enable you to stand. For many will be tossed to and fro, men's hearts shall fail them because of trouble on every hand. These days shall be very terrible, the likes of which have never been seen before.

## COMING GLORY AND DECEIVING SPIRITS

When I visit My people in mighty revival power, it is to prepare them for the darkness ahead. With the glory shall come great darkness, for the glory is to prepare My people for the darkness. I will enable My people to go through the darkness because of the visitation of My Spirit. Take heed to yourselves lest you be puffed up and think that you have arrived. Many shall be puffed up as in the olden days, for then, many received My message but they did not continue in it. Did I anoint Jehu? Yet the things that I desired were not accomplished in his life. Listen to the messengers, but do not hold men's persons in admiration or adulation. For many whom I shall anoint mightily with signs and miracles shall become lifted up and shall fall by the wayside. I do not do this willingly for I have made provision that they might stand. I call many into this ministry and equip them, but remember that many shall fall. They shall be like bright lights and the people shall delight in them. But they shall be taken over by deceiving spirits and shall lead many of My people astray. Hearken diligently concerning these things, for in the last days shall come seducing spirits. They shall turn many of My anointed ones away, many shall fall through diverse lusts and because of 'sin abounding'.

But if you will seek Me diligently I will put My Spirit within you so that when one shall turn to the right hand or to the left hand you shall not turn with them, but instead you will keep your eyes fixed wholly on your Lord. The coming days are going to be most dangerous, difficult and dark for there shall be a mighty outpouring of My Spirit in judgment upon many cities and many shall be destroyed. My people must be diligently warned concerning the days ahead. Many shall turn after seducing spirits, and already many are seducing My people. It is those who 'Do Righteousness' that are righteous. Many cover their sins by great theological words. But I warn you of seducing spirits who instruct my people in an evil way. Many of these I will anoint that they in turn may purify and sift My people, for I will have a holy people. When I come I shall not find faith upon the earth but in a few, for when the time of testing comes many will depart from their Lord.

Many shall come with seducing spirits and hold out lustful enticements. You will find that after I have visited My people again the way will become more and more narrower, and fewer shall walk therein. Be not deceived, the ways of righteousness are My ways. For though Satan come as an angel of light hearken not to him; for those who perform miracles and speak not righteousness are not of Me. I warn you with great intensity that I am going to judge My house and have a Church without spot or wrinkle when I come. I desire to open your eyes and give you spiritual understanding, that you may not be deceived, but may walk with uprightness of heart before Me, loving righteousness and hating every evil way. Look unto Me and I will make you to perceive with the eyes of the Spirit the things that lurk in darkness, that are not visible to the human eye. Let Me lead you in this way, that you may perceive the powers of darkness and battle against them. It is not a battle against flesh and blood, for if you battle in that way you accomplish nothing. But if you let Me take over and battle against the powers of darkness then they are defeated, and then liberation is brought to My people.

## THE WAY OF DECEIVERS

I warn you to search the Scriptures diligently concerning these last days. For the things that are written shall indeed be made manifest. There shall come deceivers among My people in increasing numbers, who shall speak forth the truth and shall gain the favor of the people. For the people shall examine the Scriptures and say, 'What these men say is true'. Then when they have gained the hearts of the people, then and then only shall they bring out their wrong doctrines. Therefore I say that you should not give your hearts to men, nor hold people's persons in admiration or adulation. For by these very persons Satan shall gain entry into My people. Watch for seducers! Do you think a seducer will brandish a heresy and flaunt it before the people? He will speak words of righteousness and truth and will appear as a minister of light, declaring the Word. The people's hearts shall be won. Then when the hearts are won, they will bring out their doctrines and the people shall be deceived. The people shall say 'Did he not speak thus and thus'? 'And did we not examine it from the Word'? 'Therefore he is a minister of righteousness. This that he has now spoken we do not see in the Word, but it must be right, for the other things he spoke were true'.

Be not deceived. For the deceiver will first work to gain the hearts of many, and then shall bring forth his insidious doctrines. You cannot discern those who are of Me and those who are not of Me when they start to preach. But seek Me constantly, and when these doctrines are brought out you shall have a witness in your heart that these are not of Me. Fear not, for I have warned you. It is possible that the very elect may be deceived. But it is not possible if you walk in holiness and uprightness before the Lord, for then your eyes shall be open and the Lord will protect you. If you will constantly look unto the Lord you will know when the doctrine changes, and will not be brought into it. If your heart is right I will keep you, if you will look constantly to Me, I will uphold you.

The minister of righteousness shall be on this wise—his life shall agree with the word, and his lips shall give forth that which is wholly true; there will be no mixture. When the mixture appears then you will know he is not a minister of righteousness. The deceivers speak first the truth and then error, to cover their own sins, which they love. Therefore I exhort and command you to study the Scriptures relative to seducing spirits, for this is one of the great dangers of these last days.

I desire you to be firmly established in My Word and not in the personalities of men that you will not be moved as so many shall be moved. I would keep you in the paths of righteousness. Take heed to yourselves and follow not the seducing spirits that are already manifesting themselves. Diligently inquire of Me when you hear something that you have not seen in the Word, and do not hold people's persons in admiration, for it is by this very method that Satan will hold many of My people.

## THE WAY OF TRIUMPH

I have come that you might have life and have it more abundantly, that you may triumph where I triumphed. On the cross I triumphed over all the powers of Satan and I have called you to walk in the same path. It is when your life is on the cross that you shall know the victory that I have experienced. As you are on the cross, seated in Me, then you shall know the power of the resurrection. When I come in My glory the principalities and powers in the heavenly places shall be utterly broken. Fear not, for I have given you the power whereby you may tread down the powers of darkness, and come forth victorious through every trial. As you are on the cross then you are victorious. It was on the cross that I triumphed over all the powers of the enemy. My life shall flow through as you enter into these precious truths. Look unto Me and appropriate My life. As your eyes and desires are toward Me, and you know what it is to be crucified with Me, then you shall live and your anointing shall increase. It was not in My life as I walked upon the earth, but rather it was in My life as I hung upon the cross that I openly spoiled principalities and powers.

I am showing you truth that shall cause you to overcome, to have power over the wicked one; this is the truth that will liberate you and those around you. You shall know also the fellowship of My sufferings. There is no other way whereby you may partake of this heavenly glory and to reign with Me. My Word says that if we suffer with Him we shall reign with Him. I desire to make these truths real within you. As you keep them before you, you will in turn liberate many who are in bondage. You will have revelation of those who are in darkness and will have the keys to liberate the captives. Many seek to liberate but do not have the keys. Upon the cross continually you will know the power of My resurrection.

If you will indeed judge yourself you shall not be judged. As you seek My face and desire to be cleansed by Me in all truth and sincerity of heart, I will judge you in the secret place, and the things that are in the secret place of your heart shall not be made manifest to others. I will do it in the secret place and no man will know it. The shame that will be seen on many faces shall not be seen on your face. Therefore in mercy and love I am instructing you in order that you may partake of My glory. As you are willing to walk with Me and rejoice in your sufferings, you shall in turn partake of My glory. Look unto Me for you have need of power to overcome the wicked one and the bondages in other's lives.

I said that if a man will judge himself he shall not be judged. It is not My good pleasure that the shame of My people be seen by all. How can I judge the world if I judge not first My own house? Hearken unto these things that I am telling you, for if you will not hearken unto Me thy shame shall be evident to all.

## GOD'S PART AND OUR PART

I would have you consider My life on earth—the anointing upon Me was great and yet the temptations were great on every side; they came in one form and then in another, offering Me first the glory of the kingdoms of the earth and then in the form of reviling and persecution. There will be great glory given to My people but also the temptations will be intensified on every side. Think not that with the glory there shall be no temptations or persecutions. The glory to My church shall be great and so also the temptations from the enemy to turn My people from My paths. I warn you again that when the glory shall be manifested the temptations shall be great until very few that started shall finish the course. First of all they shall be offered great worldly possessions and then will come great reviling and unbelief.

Consider your Lord, that as He walked so it shall be for you. There shall be need of great intensity of purpose. At times it will seem that everyone is rising up against you, trying to turn you from the course that I have set for you. It is written of Me that I set my face as flint to go in the direction that My Father had prescribed for Me. If you will finish the course the Lord has laid down for you, you too will have to set your face as a flint. With great determination you must walk in the course laid down for you. Many of your loved ones and those who follow with you will seek to persuade you and try to turn you from the course. With many words that seem right in the natural they will speak to you. Did not Christ rebuke Peter who would turn Him from the course God had prescribed?

Understand these two things and meditate upon them solemnly—the persecution and the darkness shall be as great as the glory in order to try to turn the elect and the anointed ones from the path the Lord has laid down for them. Many shall start but few shall be able to finish because of the greatness of grace that shall be needed to be able to endure unto the end. The temptation and the persecution of your Lord were continuous. He was tempted by Satan in many forms throughout His entire life and even to the cross where the ungodly cried out 'if thou be the Christ come down from the cross'. Think not that there will be a time of no persecution, for it shall be from the time of your anointing until the end. Difficulties and great persecution will go on to the end. The Lord must prepare you to be an overcomer in all things, that you may be able to finish the course. The persecution shall increase even as the anointing shall increase.

In paths of judgment and righteousness shall the Lord God lead His people and bring them into that place which He has chosen for them. The Lord has chosen a place for His people, a place of righteousness and holiness where He shall encamp around them. All who will be led of the Lord will be brought into this holy place. For the Lord delights to dwell in His people and to manifest Himself through His people. The holiness of the Lord will be manifested through His people. Let the Lord lead you and He will lead you in the difficult places. He led His people of old through a place where no man dwelt, where no man passed through, in a place of great danger and in the shadow of death. The Lord will indeed lead His people again through such places, and at the same time will bring them out into a place of great glory. Understand that the way toward the glory is fraught with great danger and many shall fall to the right or the left, many shall camp on lesser ground. But the Lord has a place of holiness and no unclean thing shall dwell among His people.

Put your trust in Him and He will bring you into a place of holiness. He desires to bring His people into a great glory—the likes of which has never been seen, for this is what the Lord will do for those who put their trust in Him. It is a place of darkness and great danger and it will separate His people into the place where He would have them walk. He will protect them from the voices that would turn them from His path. He will bring them through the dark places and treacherous paths and lead them out into the light of His glory. He will rejoice greatly over His beloved and cause them to be filled with joy unspeakable. He seeks to lead His people into a new place of grace and glory where He will indeed encamp among them. Put your trust in Him and He will surely bring you into this new place.

Fear not the days to come, but fear this only—that you shall walk in a manner pleasing to the Lord. In this time I am ordering and setting up My church and it shall indeed be pure, without spot or wrinkle. I will do a work in My beloved that has not been seen since the foundation of the world. I have shown you these things that you may seek the Lord diligently with all your heart, and that you may be a preserver of His people.

Run not to this one or that one for the Lord has so ordained that salvation is in Him and in Him alone. You shall not turn to this shepherd or to that one, for there shall be a great scattering upon the earth. Therefore look unto Him for He will indeed make these things clear to you. You shall not look here or there, for His wells shall increase your strength and your faith as He prepares you for the times that are coming.

The truths that I have revealed to you must become a part of you—not just an experience, but a part of your very nature. Is it not written that I demand truth in the inward parts? It is the truth of the Lord expressed in your very being that shall hold you. Many shall experience the truth but the truth must become a part of you, your very life. As men and women look upon you they will hear not only the voice but see the expression of the truth. Many shall be overcome because they are not constant in My ways and because they have not permitted the truths to become a part of them. I am showing you these things that you may be prepared, and having done all, to stand."

These prophecies and visions are filled with warnings, which otherwise have been missing in this post-modern Christian era, but are so prevalent in New Testament writings.

## NEW TESTAMENT WARNINGS

*"Beware of false prophets, who come to you in sheep's clothing, but inwardly they are ravenous wolves"* (Matthew 7:15).

*"But beware of men, for they will deliver you up to councils and scourge you in their synagogues"* (Matthew 10:17).

*"Take heed that no one deceives you. For many will come in My name saying, 'I am the Christ', and will deceive many"* (Matthew 24:4-5).

*"Then many false prophets will rise up and deceive many, and because lawlessness will abound, the love of many will grow cold. But he who endures to the end shall be saved"* (Matthew 24:11-13).

*"For false Christs and false prophets will rise and show great signs and wonders to deceive if possible, even the elect"* (Matthew 24:24).

*"Then He said to them in His teaching, 'Beware of the scribes, who desire to go around in long robes, love greetings in the marketplaces, the best seats in the synagogues, and the best places at feasts, who devour widows' houses, and for a pretense make long prayers. These will receive greater condemnation'"* (Mark 12:38-40).

*"Beware of the leaven of the Pharisees, which is hypocrisy"* (Luke 12:1).

*"Take heed and beware of covetousness, for one's life does not consist in the abundance of the things he possesses"* (Luke 12:15).

*"For I know this, that after my departure savage wolves will come in among you, not sparing the flock. Also from among yourselves men will rise up, speaking perverse things, to draw away the disciples after themselves. Therefore watch, and remember that for three years I did not cease to warn everyone night and day with tears"* (Acts 20:29-31).

*"Do not be deceived. Neither fornicators, nor idolaters, nor adulterers, nor homosexuals, nor sodomites, nor thieves, nor covetous, nor drunkards, nor revilers, nor extortioners will inherit the kingdom of God."* (1 Corinthians 6:9).

*"Therefore let him who thinks he stands take heed lest he fall"* (1 Corinthians 10:12).

*"But I fear, lest somehow, as the serpent deceived Eve by his craftiness, so your minds may be corrupted from the simplicity that is in Christ"* (1 Corinthians 11:3).

*"Do not be deceived, God is not mocked; for whatever a man sows, that shall he also reap"* (Galatians 6:7).

*"Let no one deceive you with empty words, for because of these things the wrath of God comes upon the sons of disobedience"* (Ephesians 5:6).

*"Beware of dogs, beware of evil workers, beware of the mutilation"* (Philippians 3:2).

*"For many walk, of whom I have told you often, and now tell you even weeping, that they are the enemies of the cross of Christ"* (Philippians 3:18).

*"Him we preach, warning every man and teaching every man..."* (Colossians 1:28).

*"Beware lest anyone cheat you through philosophy and empty deceit, according to the tradition of men, according to the basic principles of the world, and not according to Christ"* (Colossians 2:8).

*"Take heed to yourself and to the doctrine. Continue in them, for in doing this you will save both yourself and those who hear you"* (1 Timothy 4:16).

*"Therefore we must give the more earnest heed to the things we have heard, lest we drift away"* (Hebrews 2:1).

*"Therefore, since a promise remains of entering His rest, let us fear lest any of you seem to have come short of it"* (Hebrews 4:1).

*"Therefore, brethren, be even more diligent to make your call and election sure"* (2 Peter 1:10).

*"You therefore, beloved, since you know this beforehand, beware lest you also fall from your own steadfastness, being led away with the error of the wicked"* (2 Peter 3:17).

*"When I say unto the wicked, O wicked man, thou shalt surely die; if thou dost not speak to warn the wicked from his way, that wicked man shall die in his iniquity; but his blood I will require at your hand. Nevertheless if you warn the wicked to turn from his way, and he does not turn from his way, he shall die in his iniquity; but you have delivered your soul"* (Ezekiel 33:8-9).

# CHAPTER 21

# Nuggets of Revival and the Hope for a Third Awakening

(A majority of the content in this final chapter was taken from my studies on the outpourings and awakenings of the past. Especially useful in this endeavor was the book on Revival—Principles to Change the World, compiled by Winkie Pratney. This chapter, mainly written in my own words, is basically a synopsis of the high points of his scholarly book, which itself is filled with a multitude of quotes and references from many other books. The revival nuggets are based on observations I made from my studies. Pratney's compilation is one of the most thorough and comprehensive studies of the history of revival that I've ever read. I highly recommend this book to every saint, especially the younger generation, so that they might appreciate their spiritual heritage and learn and build on the faith of our forefathers.)

The great need of each new generation is to have a sense of both their spiritual history and divine destiny. The modern Church has little realization and appreciation of the past mighty deeds and demonstrations of God's character, glory, and power. And that lack of knowledge often hinders her from reaching for her present purpose, future destiny, and possessing a burden and a hunger for more of these mighty outpourings and awakenings.

I trust that this book will especially challenge the young to pray and give themselves for revival and a spiritual revolution in their times. When God's intervention is witnessed in the normal affairs of men there is both a manifestation of His awesome holiness and irresistible power. This results in the reviving of the Church, an awakening of the masses, and all those affected being thrust into the harvest fields of humanity.

Yet it must be stated that revival and the operation of its outpourings does not fall on an unprepared people. People must be willing and ready to pay the price of waiting on God in prayer and intercession. It usually begins with a God-given burden that leads to a great humility, a bowing down and a surrender of your own rights, a renunciation of all sin and selfish living, and a daily taking up of one's cross. One of the greatest revival scriptures in this light is 2 Chronicles 7:14:

*"If My people, who are called by My name shall humble themselves, and pray and seek My face, and turn from their wicked ways, then I will hear from heaven, and forgive their sin, and heal their land."*

This is the reason revival is unpopular with the majority of the Church. It is not the happy magical thrill that many have thought it to be with comfort, ease, and prosperity as its central piece. Thus also the reason I've included some of these themes in this book.

What I have mostly learned from my study on revivals is that we stand on the shoulders of those who have paid the price to birth and carry revival in their generation. For example, many of the Scriptural truths that were lost throughout generations of time were picked up one by one through the efforts of God's chosen vessels.

My studies on revival always begin with the Reformation when Martin Luther picked up the truth of justification by faith that had been lost. Then the themes of holiness and sanctification were picked up by champions of revival like John Wesley, Jonathan Edwards, and Charles Finney. The baptism of the Holy Ghost was restored in greater fullness at the turn of the 20th century through outpourings such as the Welch and Azusa Street revivals that spread around the world.

Then the truth of healing and miracles was given greater emphasis through the individual ministries of men such as Smith Wigglesworth and John G. Lake, and through others during the healing revival in America from 1947–1958. That revival opened things up for some of the largest attended miracle services that came after. The devil responded with the counter-culture revolution of drugs, free love, abandoned immorality and the riots of the 1960's. Into this vacuum again, as always seems to be the pattern, swept widespread awakenings such as the Jesus movement and the Charismatic renewal that impacted traditional churches and mainline denominations alike.

So many large ministries were birthed in the second half of the 20th century through the momentum that was created from such movements. Dynamic Bible schools were founded, campus ministries, the full gospel businessmen association, missions organizations like YWAM (Youth With A Mission), and Operation Mobilization among others. Television networks and ministries were established to give a wider voice to the gospel throughout America and the world.

During this era there was also a great wave of teaching that helped tie many truths together and bring personal application to them. For example, I heard the late Kenneth E. Hagin say that he would often come into an area right after Oral Roberts had been there and conduct faith and healing seminars. His teaching would help those healed in Oral Roberts miracle crusades to either recover the healing they had since lost, or to keep what they had received. Shortly before his death Smith Wigglesworth prophesied that the greatest move of God would happen in the 1980's when the teaching of the Word would be combined with the gifts and a move of the Holy Spirit. I was born again in this time and was a beneficiary of this wave of renewal and revival.

Personally, it seems that since then, the power of God has waned mostly because of an attachment to man's wisdom and methods, as the Lord has witnessed to me during recent times. The Pensacola outpouring called the Brownsville revival, of which I was familiar with and became a part of, was an instrumental and timely outpouring that helped to restore the fire of God with a renewed emphasis on repentance and holiness, which the Church seemed to have forgotten and sorely needed at the time, and frankly, still does.

Take note of what Charles Finney said in relation to this:

*"People are spiritually sluggish. So many things lead their minds away from God and oppose the influence of the gospel that God must arouse excitement in them until the wave rises so high that it sweeps away all obstacles. Before they will obey God, people must be thoroughly awakened. Only then will they overcome counteracting forces.*

*"Worldly desires, appetites, and feelings prevent true Christianity—the human will is, in a sense, enslaved by fleshly and worldly desires. It is therefore necessary for God to awaken people to a sense of guilt and danger, and thus produce an opposite excitement of feeling and desire. This counter-feeling breaks the power of worldly desire and leaves the will free to obey God."*

Very few ministers in our day would adhere to a philosophy like that. In our modern day I believe holiness, sanctification, and consecration is definitely one of the missing pieces and truths we've let go of from past generations. The body of Christ needs to pick that up. The recent overemphasis on hyper-grace has certainly not helped that cause. It has taken the glory from the vitally important theme of holiness and put it into another ditch and caused many professing Christians to do as they please.

Due to the lack of consecration and sanctification in movements like the Charismatic renewal and the widespread teaching of unscriptural doctrines, the name of Christ has been reproached as the sins and moral failures of many ministers were exposed.

**REVIVAL NUGGET:** We need to learn a lesson from the revivalists of the first and second awakenings. They built on the strengths of what was restored during the Reformation, while at the same time correcting some of the weaknesses and receiving new light and wisdom from God. With conviction they embraced the absolute authenticity and inspiration of the Scriptures on such vital themes as justification by faith, the Lordship of Jesus Christ, and the sovereignty of God. Additionally, they also picked up from their Puritan spiritual forefathers the necessity of personal holiness and discipline in the true convert.

Although no generation can master all God has for the Church of their time and era, they can learn as the revivalists of old did and go a step further than their spiritual ancestors were able to go. Many neglected and discarded themes of the gospel were restored and magnified through their efforts. Somehow I believe that a majority of our generation has dropped the baton.

There has been an all-out demonic assault of violence, corruption, immorality, and perversion on our nation and the body of Christ. Many churches have compromised the Word of God and lowered their standards. Others have simply discarded or understated certain vital themes and major truths. There is now a widespread departure from the faith as the Scriptures tell us (1 Timothy 4:1) that is unprecedented. The Supreme Court has voted to legalize gay marriage nation-wide and entire denominations have accepted it and are now endorsing same-sex marriages and ordaining gay clergy. A sewer has opened up its mouth in America, and the filth running from it is permeating our society.

We need a third awakening to restore sanity, righteousness, and morality in our nation and other nations as well. But judgment must begin in the house of God (1 Peter 4:17). The Church must get right. We must judge ourselves.

Not only have foundational truths and vital themes been restored during times of past revivals and awakenings, but the moral climate of cities, communities, and even whole nations have been changed.

For example, during the Northampton, Massachusetts revival that was ignited in 1734 when Jonathan Edwards preached his famous sermon, *"Sinners in the Hands of an Angry God,"* it was recorded that many of the hearers were seen unconsciously holding themselves up against the pillars in the church and the sides of the pews as though they already felt themselves sliding into the pit. This holy conviction spread until it affected the entire community, region, and country and came to be known as *The Great Awakening.*

Charles G. Finney, when conducting a revival near Antwerp, New York more than a century later in what became known as *The Second Great*

*Awakening,* described this same type of conviction: *"An awful solemnity seemed to settle upon the people; the congregation began to fall from their seats in every direction and cry for mercy. If I had a sword in each hand, I could not have cut them down as fast as they fell. I was obliged to stop preaching."* That conviction also spread and became a common theme of Finney's revivals and helped change entire communities as well as our nation.

As I stated earlier, an overwhelming sense of the presence of God and a deep conviction of sin seems to be a common feature of many of the older revivals. Even after the more recent outpourings of the 20th century and the many outstanding miracle/healing crusades and ministries of that time, no one has ever been able to reproduce the retention rate of new converts with the same success that revivalists like Charles Finney and others from the earlier awakenings did. The Welch revival, for example, records that about 80% of its converts stayed true to God in their first five years. Finney had the same type of results. Although salvation was preached, it was not the emphasis of the great healing and miracle revivals and crusades of the latter century. It was a different stream.

## HOW REVIVAL CAN CHANGE A NATION'S PRESENT AND FUTURE

What comes first—judgment or revival? Often they arrive at the same time.

In the mid 1800's during the days of Charles Finney, America had sunk into great spiritual poverty, which led to a steep economic collapse. Uncannily, much like today, there were five contributing factors to that collapse.

1. **Greed**: The gap between prosperity and poverty widened attributing greatly to the increase of violent crime.

2. **Occultism**: Hungry for the supernatural the nation turned to spiritualism.

3. **Immorality**: The playboy philosophy of "free love" was endorsed and embraced by many.

4. **Political and commercial corruption**: National laws legalized the cruel use of slavery and bribes and illegal business practices were rampant.

5. **Atheism**: Agnosticism, apathy, and indifference toward God and spiritual things abounded on every hand.

This spiritual decline in our nation touched four main areas: Spiritual, moral, political, and social. Judgment came as secular and spiritual conditions combined to unravel one of the most severe economic and social crashes our nation has ever experienced. Thousands of merchants lost everything as banks failed and the railroad industry went into bankruptcy. Multitudes of people lost their jobs as factories shut down. In New York City alone there were some 30,000 men who were idle on the streets. By 1857 people were no longer looking to financially thrive and get ahead but only to eat and survive.

Many prognostics are predicting a similar crash in the very near future right here within our shores. Truly the conditions are ripe for it.

How did America recover from such tumultuous times? It was through the great revival that began in 1857, which not only helped America to recover but also laid the groundwork and set the stage for the revivals of the 20th century and that which I believe is still to come. How did it happen?

Led by inarguably the greatest evangelist and revivalist of our time, Charles Finney, and his fiery converts, these three elements helped pave the way.

1. **A burning desire to implement the message of personal holiness.** They preached and stressed a complete consecration to God that included your spouse and children, possessions and reputation, and the willingness to preach publicly.

2. **A spreading everywhere of benevolent responsibility which flowed from personal holiness and sanctification.** The revivalists linked true conversion and spiritual growth directly to the alteration of society and the culture. They never believed that isolating yourself and living in a hole would make one holy. They had a large vision of a mighty revival that would spread throughout the world and prepare mankind for the coming of the Lord.

3. **The baptism of the Holy Spirit as a vital essential and not an option.** There was a hunger for an experience that would 'make Christianity work'. The leaders of this revival were not mystic dreamers. Finney believed and preached that the theme of the baptism of the Holy Spirit was not only the secret of pulpit power but it was the fountain of energy that would evangelize the entire world.

In December of 1857 a convention on revival was called by the Presbyterians. About 200 ministers and many laity gathered, as much of the time was spent in prayer. There were Baptist and Methodist pastors in New York who decided to set aside one day a week for all day prayer and intercession for an outpouring of the Holy Spirit. By the beginning of 1858 messages on revival were being preached all over the East. Prayer was such a key to the 1857 awakening that it has been called the Prayer Meeting Revival, led, organized, and conducted by many laity, which was another key element of the revival.

**REVIVAL NUGGET**: *"There is going to be a great spiritual awakening in the world, and it is going to come from plain, simple people who know—not simply believe—but actually know that God answers prayer. It is going to be a great revival of Christianity, not a revival of religion. This is going to be a revival of true Christianity. It is going to rise from the laymen, from men who are going about their work and putting God into what they do, from men who believe in prayer, and who want to make God real to mankind."*—George Washington Carver

Consider these other amazing prophetic quotes on the significance of lay people in revivals.

*"God gave me a revelation of the last days. It is the laymen that will reach the world."* He went on to call laymen *"the sleeping giant of evangelism."*—Mordecai Hamm (the minister who led Billy Graham to the Lord)

*"Laymen will be His most important channel—not the clergy, or the theologians, or the great gifted preachers, but men and women with ordinary jobs in the ordinary world."*—Charles Price

*"If this world is going to be reached, I am convinced that it must be done by men and women of average talent."*—Dwight L. Moody

*"God is going to take the do-nothings, the nobodies, the unheard-of, the no-accounts... He is going to take every man and every woman and he is going to give to them this outpouring of the Spirit of God."*
—Tommy Hicks

In 1857 when many began seeing the desperate situation in the city and country, ads for a noon day prayer meeting on Wednesday were passed out in downtown New York. The meetings began with few in attendance but grew steadily until they decided to meet daily instead of weekly.

Within 6 months over 10,000 businessmen were meeting every day in similar meetings, confessing sin, getting saved, and praying for revival. People met in stores, company buildings, and churches. Doctrinal controversies and jealousies were put to the side as churches began to pray and work together as one.

The amazing result was that America came back from the dead and in just two years' time one million converts were added to all denominational churches. The social and ethical effects continued for almost half a century. This revival spread across the ocean to Great Britain, Scotland, Ireland, and Wales with approximately two million converts added to the churches in those nations.

Some great and influential ministries were birthed during this period of time and era of revival. Such examples included the blossoming ministry of D.L. Moody and Ira Sankey, William and Catherine Booth and the Salvation Army, Hudson Taylor's revival based concept of interdenominational missions, the China Inland Mission, and many others.

What can we learn and glean today from this great revival and awakening? We can be encouraged that true revival can change the moral climate of a community and a nation. When God finds a people who have the will and spirit to pray, the courage to preach, and live a life of consecration and holiness combined with compassion and outreach He can really begin to work. The hand and touch of God on ordinary people wholly consecrated to Him can make a huge difference.

Some might be of the persuasion that it's too late for America. It's too dark; it's too far gone; it's too sick. But let me remind you of a great principle of revival and compare it to a hurricane.

Meteorologists can forecast the strength of the winds in a developing hurricane by the atmospheric pressure. I've never studied meteorology but as I understand it, the disparity of atmospheric pressure between the sea and the air creates a vacuum. The greater the vacuum the more violent will be the winds and the greater the water evaporation. For example, every inch of reduction in atmospheric pressure results in 13 more inches of water being lifted up by the hurricane as it acts as a vacuum cleaner. The water and the winds are what create devastation and destruction in a hurricane.

There is a great vacuum of despair, darkness, and death in our culture right now. There is a great God vacuum of true spirituality, which means hope springs eternal for an intense spiritual hurricane that could produce the biggest spiritual waves any generation has ever seen yet. One of those waves could be the very one that brings Jesus back to the earth and takes us right into the shores of heaven to close out the Church age. Hallelujah!

**REVIVAL NUGGET**: Civic controversies such as same sex marriage are not new to American life and culture. Back in the 1800's there was slavery, in the 1900's there was abortion and prison reform. It is the responsibility of the Church to confront these issues and the moral conscience of the culture in any nation. Times like these of gross darkness and immorality call for a restoration of that godly mandate—a message that both expects and demands personal and practical holiness from individual members in the body of Christ and biblical repentance from the community.

The modern version of repentance calls for almost no personal change, no personal sacrifice, and no renunciation of any kind. An improved lifestyle is mostly what we offer—using God to fulfill your personal dream of success, whatever that means to you. Religious people and sinners hate the message of biblical repentance but they love the modern version and we seem to cater to them. Thus, counterfeit conversion has become the order of the day. Churches are filled with false converts. Holiness and heart purity is not an option but an essential for young converts. Revivals of the past especially those of the first and second awakenings were brought to birth and escalated by this divine principle.

## THE 20TH CENTURY AWAKENING

As great of an awakening as the 1857 revival was, history records that the most impactful revivals were the international outpourings at the turn of the 20th century. It was decades later that scholars and historians were able to properly assess how powerful those outpourings were. Revivals were happening simultaneously 10,000 miles apart in India, the Far East, Africa, Latin America, and in islands like Bermuda. Everyone seemed to be moved to pray at the same time. There were

South Pacific awakenings in Australia and New Zealand as well. And of course, in Los Angeles, California of the United States the highly documented Azusa Street revival was birthed and spread across our nation as well. But historians say that no outpouring had the widest and most felt impact that the Welch revival did.

When a young reporter came to Wales to witness the amazing outpouring he asked Evan Roberts if he had a message for America. After quoting Joel 2:28 of the promise of God to pour out the Holy Spirit on all flesh, Roberts simply told him that all flesh must be ready. But then he said that four conditions must be observed as essentials:

1. The past must be clear, and every sin confessed to God, and any wrong done to man must be made right.

2. Everything doubtful must be removed once and for all out of our lives. Is there anything in your life you cannot decide whether it is good or evil? Away with it. There must not be a trace of a cloud between you and God.

3. There must be prompt, implicit, unquestioning obedience to the Spirit of God. At whatever cost, do what the Holy Spirit prompts you to do without hesitation or fear.

4. Make public confession of Christ.

We would do well to heed Evan Roberts' words of wisdom if we expect the same results.

The churches in Wales were crowded for two years with 100,000 outsiders being converted. Drunkenness was reduced by 50%, taverns went bankrupt, crime nearly disappeared so that judges had no more cases to judge, and the police became unemployed in many districts. This outpouring affected all nations. It spread like wild fire through Ireland and Scotland, and into other nations of Europe where meetings were marked by prayer and confession of sin.

It is phenomenal to read about how far reaching the turn of last century's outpourings were. It was not only international but ecumenical as well; it impacted major nations and involved major churches and denominations such as the Baptists, Lutherans, Methodists, Presbyterians, Anglicans, Congregationalists, Disciple, and Reformed churches. The only ones left virtually untouched as in earlier awakenings were the Roman Catholic and Greek Orthodox communities.

It is recorded that William T. Stead, a London newspaper editor, considered by some to be the most powerful man in Britain at that time, gave this impression of the Wales revival.

*"There is something there from another world. You cannot say whence it came or whither it is going, but it moves and lives and reaches for you all the time. You see men and women go down in sobbing agony before your eyes as the invisible Hand clutches at their heart. And you shudder."*

When asked if it was all emotion and if there was any teaching, Stead responded:

*"Precious little. Do you think teaching is what people want in a revival? These people, all the people in a land like ours are taught to death, preached to insensibility. They all know the essential truths. They know they are not living as they ought to live, and no amount of teaching will add anything to that conviction."*

This is where we presently are as a Church today.

It takes a man of wisdom and understanding to know the times and seasons of God, and what the Spirit is calling for. Teaching is important, but there are times when people will never abandon their sin and idolatry unless they are aroused and awakened until they cannot contain themselves. When Christianity degenerates and the Church backslides, the nation is further darkened and sucked down into gross immorality, perversion, pride, greed, and idolatry. It takes these awakenings to revive and promote Christianity.

**REVIVAL NUGGET:** There are two elements that often lead to revival: Spiritual hunger and/or a great crisis. Prayer is often born from these two elements. And the two foundation stones that make it all work are the preparedness of man and the sovereignty of God.

God has always worked throughout history by means of revival. The fallen nature of human beings in cooperation with the devil tend to evil and sliding off into Deism, and God has to often reverse this downward cycle through sudden and mighty outpourings of His Spirit, sometimes preceded by judgments.

*"Then the Lord saw that the wickedness of man was great in the earth, and that every intent of the thoughts of his heart was only evil continually"* (Genesis 6:5).

God always looks for a man to stand in the gap and plead for the sins of the people. He found such a man in Noah (Genesis 6:8). This has always been the case throughout Israel's history that God raised up a leader in a time of judgment and brought restoration. From Abraham to Moses to Gideon to Jephthah; from Jehosaphat to Hezekiah to Josiah it has always been the pattern.

We are facing the same cycle today as Israel and our spiritual forefathers did before us. There is first a cycle of idolatry and decay, then reformation and revival, and then a gradual backsliding into apostasy again, which follows the four fold collapse of Israel's history:

1. Israel forgot God.

2. Israel forgot God's laws.

3. Israel made up new gods.

4. Israel made up new laws.

Nations leave the ways of God because of a physical law present in the universe called, the Second Law of Thermodynamics. Basically this law teaches us that things tend to run down, not up; from order and cohesion to disorder and decay and eventually death. This is the reason reforms, revivals, and awakenings are mandatory. They create spiritual momentum and violent upheavals in society.

For example, The Renaissance and Protestant Reformation in the 15th century changed the whole thought and life of Europe that modern history still dates back from them.

The great missionary movements of the 19th century derived its momentum from the great revivals in America and Britain during those times. Also, many of the evangelistic explosions in many third world countries today trace back to that time.

In light of the abominable sins of our modern culture and the widespread deception and apostasy of a backslidden church, oh, how we need a third great awakening right now that will affect not only America, but the nations of the world! May God grant it as His people prepare for it.

## SOME FINAL THOUGHTS

Revival is the operation of divine impulse. It cannot be worked up. *"There came a sound from heaven"* (Acts 2:2). Similar to salvation it is based on the grounds of grace, and the fulfilled conditions are repentance, faith, and prayer. There is a spontaneity about it and has the power to continue unabated without the help of man and the arm of flesh. As soon as it becomes controlled or organized and stops being spontaneous it is no longer considered a revival.

The spirit and manifestation of revival is intensely personal. You feel as if God is speaking directly to you. He comes for you and calls your name. There is an overwhelming God-consciousness—*"they were pricked in their heart"* (Acts 2:37); and *"fear came on every soul"* (Acts 2:43). In revival men are suddenly aware of God's irresistible power (the sound of a mighty rushing wind) and His awesome holiness (divine appearances of tongues of fire), and their souls come under His grip.

During times of revival there is a fresh emphasis of the person and work of the Holy Spirit. *"And they were all filled with the Holy Spirit"* (Acts 2:4). The sound of revival and the power of God draws people into it; *"the multitude came together"* (Acts 2:6), and the miracle of it amazes them—*"they were all amazed and marveled"* (Acts 2:7). And it causes curious onlookers to say to one another, *"what does this mean?"* (Acts 2:12).

Peter's preaching came from the outpouring (Acts 2:14) and then the outpouring came from his preaching (Acts 2:37-38). When a church is backslidden and a nation is far from God repentance is always the aim of true revival. The question of sin must be faithfully dealt with that the conscience might be stirred and aroused.

**REVIVAL NUGGET:** I believe that the coming apostolic ministries of our day will be carriers of true revival. Like Stephen of old (Acts 6:8-10) they will be full of faith and power and do great wonders and signs among the people, while speaking with an irresistible wisdom and Spirit. This combination of the deeply convicting repentance preaching of one like Charles Finney and the daring, miracle-working faith of Smith Wigglesworth will bring a mighty apostolic anointing and authority that has been lacking in recent times. It will ignite the common man to carry that witness into the marketplace.

Preachers and people often complain that sin and pleasure-loving sinners are hardened and won't come to hear the gospel. Large sums of money may be spent on publicity and advertising with little results. But where natural means fail to produce the desired results, we must look to the Spirit of God and His supernatural workings.

When Elijah questioned the people with, *"How long will you falter between two opinions?"* the people were silent and refused to answer (1 Kings 18:21). But then when God sent the fire, the people instantly fell on their faces. *"Now when the people saw it, they fell on their faces; and they said, 'The Lord, He is God! The Lord, He is God!'* What the efforts of men cannot achieve God is able to achieve in a moment of time through the outpouring of the Spirit.

That has always been and always will be the Church's only hope.

May the *"God who answers by fire"* manifest His glory and make the people fall on their faces and turn their hearts to Him again.

# *Holiness Scriptures*

*Blessed are the pure in heart, for they shall see God.* (Matthew 5:8)

*You are the salt of the earth; but if the salt loses its flavor, how shall it be seasoned? It is then good for nothing but to be thrown out and trampled underfoot by men. You are the light of the world. A city that is set on a hill cannot be hidden. Nor do they light a lamp and put it under a basket, but on a lampstand, and it gives light to all who are in the house. Let your light so shine before men, that they may see your good works and glorify your Father in heaven.* (Matthew 5:13-16)

*What then? Shall we sin because we are not under law but under grace? By no means! Don't you know that when you offer yourselves to someone to obey him as slaves, you are slaves to the one whom you obey—whether you are slaves to sin, which leads to death, or to obedience, which leads to righteousness? But thanks be to God that, though you used to be slaves to sin, you wholeheartedly obeyed the form of teaching to which you were entrusted. You have been set free from sin and have become slaves to righteousness. I put this in human terms because you are weak in your natural selves. Just as you used to offer the parts of your body in slavery to impurity and to ever-increasing wickedness, so now offer them in slavery to righteousness leading to holiness. When you were slaves to sin, you were free from the control of righteousness. What benefit did you reap at that time from the things you are now ashamed of? Those things result in death! But now that you have been set free from sin and have become slaves to God, the benefit you reap leads to holiness, and the result is eternal life. For the wages of sin is death, but the gift of God is eternal life in Christ Jesus our Lord.* (**Romans 6:15-23**) From slaves of sin to slaves of righteousness

*And do not be conformed to this world, but be transformed by the renewing of your mind, that you may prove what is that good and acceptable and perfect will of God.* (**Romans 12:2**)

*I wrote to you in my epistle not to keep company with sexually immoral people. Yet I certainly did not mean with the sexually immoral people of this world, or with the covetous, or extortioners, or idolaters, since then you would need to go out of the world. But now I have written to you not to keep company with anyone named a brother, who is sexually immoral, or covetous, or an idolater, or a reviler, or a drunkard, or an extortioner—not even to eat with such a person. For what have I to do with judging those also who are outside? Do you not judge those who are inside? But those who are outside God judges. Therefore "put away from yourselves the evil person."* (**1 Corinthians 5:9-13**) What would the evangelical church of America look like if we practiced this today? How many would be left?

*Do you not know that the unrighteous will not inherit the kingdom of God? Do not be deceived. Neither fornicators, nor idolaters, nor adulterers, nor homosexuals, nor sodomites, nor thieves, nor covetous, nor*

*drunkards, nor revilers, nor extortioners will inherit the kingdom of God. And such were some of you. But you were washed, but you were sanctified, but you were justified in the name of the Lord Jesus and by the Spirit of our God.* (**1 Corinthians 6:9-11**) REAL CHANGE

*And what agreement has the temple of God with idols? For you are the temple of the living God. As God has said: "I will dwell in them and walk among them. I will be their God, and they shall be My people." Therefore "Come out from among them and be separate, says the Lord. Do not touch what is unclean, and I will receive you."* (**2 Corinthians 6:16-17**)

*Therefore, having these promises, beloved, let us cleanse ourselves from all filthiness of the flesh and spirit, perfecting holiness in the fear of God.* (**2 Corinthians 7:1**)

*Just as He chose us in Him before the foundation of the world, that we should be holy and without blame before Him in love...* (**Ephesians 1:4**)

*For you were once darkness, but now you are light in the Lord. Walk as children of light.* (**Ephesians 5:8**) From darkness to light

*Husbands, love your wives, as Christ loved the church and gave Himself up for her, so that He might sanctify her, having cleansed her by the washing of water with the Word, that He might present the church to Himself in glorious splendor, without spot or wrinkle or any such things [that she might be holy and faultless.]* (**Ephesians 5:25-27 Amp**)

*As for you, you were dead in your transgressions and sins, in which you used to live when you followed the ways of this world and of the ruler of the kingdom of the air, the spirit who is now at work in those who are disobedient. All of us also lived among them at one time, gratifying the cravings of our sinful nature and following its desires and thoughts. Like the rest, we were by nature objects of wrath. But because of his great love for us, God, who is rich in mercy, made us alive with Christ even when we were dead in transgressions—it is by grace you have been saved.* (**Ephesians 2:1-5**) From death to life

*Do all things without complaining and disputing, that you may become blameless and harmless, children of God without fault in the midst of a crooked and perverse generation, among whom you shine as lights in the world, holding fast the word of life, so that I may rejoice in the day of Christ that I have not run in vain or labored in vain.* (**Philippians 2:14-16**)

*For he has rescued us from the dominion of darkness and brought us into the kingdom of the Son he loves...* (**Colossians 1:13**) Translated from one kingdom to another

*If then you were raised with Christ, seek those things which are above, where Christ is, sitting at the right hand of God. Set your mind on things above, not on things on the earth. For you died, and your life is hidden with Christ in God. When Christ who is our life appears, then you also will appear with Him in glory. Therefore put to death your members which are on the earth: fornication, uncleanness, passion, evil desire, and covetousness, which is idolatry. Because of these things the wrath of God is coming upon the sons of disobedience, in which you yourselves once walked when you lived in them. But now you yourselves are to put off all these: anger, wrath, malice, blasphemy, filthy language out of your mouth. Do not lie to one another, since you have put off the old man with his deeds, and have put on the new man who is renewed in knowledge according to the image of Him who created him... Therefore, as the elect of God, holy and beloved, put on tender mercies, kindness, humility, meekness, longsuffering; bearing with one another, and forgiving one another, if anyone has a complaint against another; even as Christ forgave you, so you also must do. But above all these things put on love, which is the bond of perfection.* (Colossians 3:1-10, 12-14)

*For God did not call us to uncleanness, but to holiness.* (1 Thessalonians 4:7)

*A bishop then must be blameless, the husband of one wife, temperate, sober-minded, of good behavior, hospitable, able to teach; Moreover he must have a good testimony among those who are outside, lest he fall into reproach and the snare of the devil.* (1 Timothy 3:2, 7) Elders are to live above reproach; it is shameful for any believer to suffer as a murderer, or thief, or a meddler, or any kind of criminal.

*For we ourselves were also once foolish, disobedient, deceived, serving various lusts and pleasures, living in malice and envy, hateful and hating one another. But when the kindness and the love of God our Savior toward man appeared, not by works of righteousness which we have done, but according to His mercy He saved us, through the washing of regeneration and renewing of the Holy Spirit, whom He poured out on us abundantly through Jesus Christ our Savior, that having been justified by His grace we should become heirs according to the hope of eternal life.* (Titus 3:3-7) REAL CHANGE

*But as He who called you is holy, you also be holy in all your conduct, because it is written, "Be holy, for I am holy."* (1 Peter 1:15-16)

*Beloved, I beg you as sojourners and pilgrims, abstain from fleshly lusts which war against the soul, having your conduct honorable among the Gentiles, that when they speak against you as evildoers, they may, by your good works which they observe, glorify God in the day of visitation.* (1 Peter 2:11-12)

*Beloved, do not think it strange concerning the fiery trial which is to try you, as though some strange thing happened to you; but rejoice to the extent that you partake of Christ's sufferings, that when His glory is revealed, you may also be glad with exceeding joy. If you are reproached for the name of Christ, blessed are you, for the Spirit of glory and of God rests upon you. On their part He is blasphemed, but on your part He is glorified. But let none of you suffer as a murderer, a thief, an evildoer, or as a busybody in other people's matters. Yet if anyone suffers as a Christian, let him not be ashamed, but let him glorify God in this matter.* (1 Peter 4:12-16) Our glory is to suffer because of our identification with Jesus

*As His divine power has given to us all things that pertain to life and godliness, through the knowledge of Him who called us by glory and virtue, by which have been given to us exceedingly great and precious promises, that through these you may be partakers of the divine nature, having escaped the corruption that is in the world through lust. But also for this very reason, giving all diligence, add to your faith virtue, to virtue knowledge, to knowledge self-control, to self-control perseverance, to perseverance godliness, to godliness brotherly kindness, and to brotherly kindness love. For if these things are yours and abound, you will be neither barren nor unfruitful in the knowledge of our Lord Jesus Christ. For he who lacks these things is shortsighted, even to blindness, and has forgotten that he was cleansed from his old sins.* (2 Peter 1:3-9)

*Therefore, since all these things will be dissolved, what manner of persons ought you to be in holy conduct and godliness...* (2 Peter 3:11)

*Pursue peace with all people, and holiness, without which no one will see the Lord...* (Hebrews 12:14)

*Now by this we know that we know Him, if we keep His commandments. He who says, "I know Him," and does not keep His commandments, is a liar, and the truth is not in him.* (1 John 2:3-4)

*He who says he abides in Him ought himself also to walk just as He walked.* (1 John 2:6)

*Whoever abides in Him does not sin. Whoever sins has neither seen Him nor known Him.* (1 John 3:6)

*Love has been perfected among us in this: that we may have boldness in the day of judgment; because as He is, so are we in this world.* (1 John 4:17)

# About the Author

Bert M. Farias, together with his wife Carolyn, graduates of Rhema Bible Training Center, founded Holy Fire Ministries in 1997 after serving for 9 years as missionaries in West Africa establishing nation-changing interdenominational Bible training centers with an organization called Living Word Missions.

From 1999–2003 Bert served as the internship coordinator on the senior leadership team of the Brownsville Revival School of Ministry and Fire School of Ministry in Pensacola, Florida, a school birthed from a massive heaven-sent revival that brought approximately four million visitors from around the world with an estimated 150,000 first time conversions. There Rev. Farias and his wife taught and mentored young men and women in the call of God and training them for the work of the ministry.

Bert is a messenger of the Lord carrying a spirit of revival to the Church and the nations. An anointing of fire marks His ministry with frequent demonstrations of the Spirit and the power of God. With a divine commission to also write, Bert has authored several books with an emphasis on helping to restore the true spirit of Christianity in the Church and preparing the saints for the glory of God, the harvest, and the soon return of the Lord.

Before being separated to the full time preaching and teaching ministry, Bert experienced a unique and powerful baptism of fire. His consuming passion is for human beings to come into a real and vibrant relationship with the Lord Jesus Christ through the power of the Holy Spirit and to become passionate workers in His kingdom, thus preparing them for the second coming of Christ, being among the wise virgins and a part of the first-fruits harvest who will gain an abundant entrance into glory and receive a sure reward.

Bert currently resides in Windham, New Hampshire with his beautiful wife Carolyn. They are proud parents of one adult son.

# Other Books by Bert M. Farias

## PRAYER: THE LANGUAGE OF THE SPIRIT

Prayer: The Language Of The Spirit is a short and poignant book that helps lay a foundation from the Word for knowing and walking with God. Each chapter directs the earnest believer into possessing a life of communion with God and praying without ceasing.

Prayer is walking with God. It is habitual fellowship with God. You can walk so close to God that you feel like you're in heaven. The key that will move you toward this richness of communion with Him is to not only know the Word but to cultivate a receptivity and sensitivity to His Spirit and presence.

You can experience this kind of life in God if you will pursue Him. It all begins with receiving the baptism of the Holy Spirit and praying extensively in other tongues. This is the LANGUAGE OF THE SPIRIT.

## MY SON, MY SON

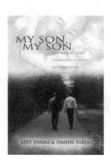

Here's a beautiful story of the miraculous fulfillment of a promised son's entrance into the world to the season of the son's departure from home—a joyful journey that takes you into the heart of a loving relationship between a father and a son.

This book is one of the most unique books on father-son relationships you will ever find. Co-written by father and son, it has a personal touch and an intimate tone that will leave you teary-eyed one moment and then rejoicing the next. Within its pages you will find a spiritual quality of training and a godly example of shepherding children that will both enrich and empower parents. It also offers hope for those parents who have fallen short or started late in their child training.

## SOULISH LEADERSHIP

This book is for everyone...

- Who longs for purity of heart.

- Who desires to be set aright in the core of his being.

- Who dreads God's disapproval more than man's.

- Whose greatest phobia is the fear of a wasted life and burned-up works.

The works that endure the testing of God's holy fire will one day be rewarded. Others will suffer loss (1 Cor 3:12-15). Will your works stand the fire or will they go up in smoke?

In that day the motive of every heart will be made clear. Leaders will judged by a higher standard. Only one question will matter then, and it's the same question that matters now: Are you building your kingdom or the kingdom of God?

## PURITY OF HEART

The primary basis of all judgment concerning the deeds done in our bodies is our motives. Our values determine our motives, and our motives are the real reason behind our thoughts, words, and deeds. Only God can see the true motives of every man's heart.

Almost all human beings have something to hide. Nearly everyone twists words, events, and situations to their own advantage, to place themselves in the best possible light. Men often have ulterior motives and hidden agendas. This is sin and a form of hiding.

Adam and Eve first hid from the presence of the Lord in the garden after they had fallen. God asked them why they ate the forbidden fruit. "Why" is the question God chose to ask them. And one day when true Christians stand before the judgment seat of Christ, this is the question that shall reveal our hearts.

Purity of Heart will prepare you for that day and spare you loss at the judgment seat of Christ so that you may receive your full reward. What is done in pure love, by the leading of the Spirit, and for the glory and honor of God shall reap the fullest rewards.

## THE JOURNAL OF A JOURNEY TO HIS HOLINESS

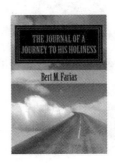

I thank my God I speak in tongues more than you all; yet in the church…" (1 Cor 14:18-19a). As the principal writer of the New Testament, the apostle

Paul's private use of speaking in tongues was his key to revelation knowledge and to his understanding of the mysteries of God. The same is true today.

This book, written in journal form, details one minister's journey of how time spent praying in other tongues gave him the needed wisdom, knowledge, and understanding of God's more perfect plan for his life.

Praying in tongues is both a purifying fire and a devouring fire. As you pray in other tongues the fire of God will devour your works of wood, hay, and stubble while at the same time purifying your works of gold, silver, and precious stones. This will save your works at the judgment seat of Christ and cause you to enter into a sure reward.

This journal is written from Spirit to spirit as deep crying unto deep. As you drink of its rich contents with an open and hungry heart there will be an unveiling of hidden secrets and a closeness of God's presence that will edify your life.

## THE REAL SALVATION

Can you imagine feeling secure in a salvation you don't even possess? Such is the state of mass humanity today. We have libraries full of sermons yet still so much confusion and deception about what the real salvation is. With poignancy and pinpoint clarity this short and sweet book cuts through the fat of satanic philosophy, exposes the deception of the broad way of religion, and shines the light on the narrow path to eternal life.

Most books are 200 pages with 30 pages worthwhile, and 170 of fluff. The Real Salvation is less than 60 pages, but every word counts. Make it count for you and your unsaved friends and loved ones!

## THE REAL GOSPEL

With piercing prophetic insight this book exposes the fallacies and shortcuts in the modern gospel and calls us back to Jesus and the cross. Its message reveals why so many Christians and churches today lack power, endurance, and character. Written in the spirit, style, and plainness of speech of the old timers, it breathes into today's shallow gospel the life of the spirit of holiness, giving us fresh eyes on old truths.

This is a critical book for the hour—a real wake up call to all. Backed by an abundance of scripture The Real Gospel is as truthful as it is radical.

*\*To order any of these books visit our website www.holy-fire.org or Amazon books.\**

To become a monthly partner with Holy Fire Ministries
or to receive the ministry's free newsletter please contact:

HOLY FIRE MINISTRIES
PO Box 4527
Windham, NH 03087
www.holy-fire.org

Holy Fire Publishing's three-fold purpose is: 1) To help restore the real spirit of Christianity in the Church. 2) Secondly, to light a fire in human spirits. 3) Thirdly, to save and deliver.

Bert M. Farias is an experienced and anointed missionary revivalist to the Church and the nations, who seeks to make disciples, not merely converts. In this book, Bert challenges the status quo of Christianity today and redefines its true spirit which is one of revival and of living the Spirit filled life. With one eye on the coming glory of the Lord and His soon return, and another eye on the harvest of souls yet to be reached, *The Real Spirit Of Revival* takes the reader into a preparation to becoming a true lover of Jesus and a passionate worker in His kingdom. These vital truths that dot each new chapter of this book are sure to awaken you as one from a deep sleep, and light a fire in your soul.

If you are tired of a mundane relationship with God and desire to burn with His holy fire this book is a must read.